The
BREAKUP
PIVOT

*A Guide to Overcoming Heartbreak
and Designing Your Best Life*

**VOLUME I
OVERCOMING HEARTBREAK**

Tanya Partee, JD

LYFE

BOOKS

THE BREAKUP PIVOT

Author's Note

The Breakup Pivot series is not intended as a substitute for treatment with a doctor or a professional therapist but is offered only as a self-help guide to understanding the grief process and identifying areas of your life that may need to be addressed in order to heal and rebound from a heartbreak. You should never delay seeking professional help or discontinue any medical treatment because of information in *The Breakup Pivot* series.

Mariah is a fictional character whose experiences are partly a composite of stories from the author's clients, family members, and friends. Mention of specific companies, businesses, organizations, or authorities in this book does not imply endorsement by the author, nor does the mention of specific companies, businesses, organization, or authorities imply that they endorse this book or its author. Internet addresses and telephone numbers given in this book were accurate at the time it went to press.

Dedication

This book is dedicated to my sister, Candyce.

Thank you for consistently being my rock through every breakup and heartache in my life and for always reminding me that "this too shall pass".

I love you!

Table of Contents

Preface

You have been prayed for, by me. Yes, **You**. I pray that everyone who picks up this book and reads it has a blessing of healing, restoration, and prosperity in their life. God has big plans for your life and every bump in the road is making you stronger for your purpose in this world. We are molded and shaped through every adversity and trial. You are much stronger than you think, and your heartbreak pain will—eventually—pass.

Why did I write *The Breakup Pivot* series?

In all transparency—I had a devasting heartbreak in my 40s by a man that I loved deeply and had invested my heart and soul in. As a result of the breakup, my self-esteem tanked, I was angry, and I was sad and lonely— which led to many crying spells in the middle of the workday behind closed doors. However, heartbreak had not been a stranger—we had met before on a few other occasions. I was betrayed in my 20s, experienced the pain of marital infidelity in my 30s, and after my divorce I experienced this last heartbreak in my 40s.

But instead of being just another heartbreak, the difference was how I decided to deal with it. I did not stuff the pain down, pretending it did not happen or that it wasn't that bad to quickly move on to the next relationship—which was how I had dealt with the pain in the past. There was a definitive moment that I got fed up with being in a rut and I got in the driver's seat of my own story. I took the time to sit in the pain and work through it. Then I took a self-inventory of my baggage, behaviors, and mindset. I realized that I had to make a pivot to head in another direction to have the life I wanted for myself.

I have been where you are and I am here to show you how to break free from unforgiveness, anxiety, fear, anger, and your self-limiting beliefs so you can experience life filled with peace, joy and success greater than ever before.

Read this book with a highlighter or the e-book highlighter option to mark the sections that resonate with you. Use this book as a hands-on resource for strength and guidance throughout your post-breakup season.

Who is *The Breakup Pivot: Overcoming Heartbreak* written for?

This book is written for you if you were in a romantic relationship which ended most likely not on your own terms and you are sad, hurt, angry, devastated, in denial, have been downgraded to a "friends with benefits" category, or have entered into "stalker-like" activities. If you are still grieving the loss of the relationship, then this book can help you overcome your heartbreak.

However, if you have been depressed (experiencing unhealthy/inconsistent eating habits, unhealthy sleep patterns, hopelessness, irritability, loss of interest or emptiness) for more than six months or are suicidal (thoughts of ending your own life), I strongly urge you to seek professional counseling or contact the **National Suicide Prevention Lifeline** at: 1-800-273-8255 *immediately*.

What is *The Breakup Pivot* series about?

A pivot is a change in strategy while keeping the same vision. *The Breakup Pivot* series is about positively changing the trajectory of the pain and heartache from your breakup while keeping the same vision of creating your best life.

You have no control over other people's actions, but you have control over your own thoughts and actions. With *The Breakup Pivot* series you will learn the tools and techniques that, if implemented and practiced, will result in a higher level of peace, joy, fulfillment, love, and success than ever before.

The Breakup Pivot series is divided into four (4) volumes to guide you through overcoming heartbreak, healing, rebuilding and designing your life:

<u>Volume I:</u> *Overcoming Heartbreak*—takes you on a journey through the phases of Heartbreak Grief: (a) Shock, (b) Denial, (c) Anger, (d) Depression, (e) Desperate for Answers and/or Contact and (f) Acceptance.

<u>Volume II:</u> *The Healing Process*—helps you with Forgiveness, Unpacking the Baggage, Overcoming Anxiety and Fear, and Ending the Sabotage Cycle.

<u>Volume III:</u> *The Rebuilding Process*—helps you with Shifting Your Mindset, Caring for Your Body and Spirit, Gratitude as the New Attitude, and Raising Your Energy Vibration.

<u>Volume IV:</u> *L.Y.F.E. by Design*—helps you with Finding Your "Why," Goal Setting, the Power of Visualization, and Mindset Mastery.

Through the life of fictional character Mariah—who has been through a recent breakup and is heartbroken—

you are taken on a journey that will help you make sense of what you are going through and get you on the path to becoming whole and the best version of yourself.

Introduction

The harsh reality is that your relationship is over. Your ex hijacked that future you had envisioned with him. I get it. I've been there too—heartbroken, angry, and sad. Now what?

If you want to spend lots of futile energy and tears trying to win your ex back, then *The Breakup Pivot* series is not for you. If you want to try to go on with your life as if nothing happened and jump into a new relationship or distraction without doing the work to heal first, then *The Breakup Pivot* series is not for you. *However,* if you want to heal, get your joy and exuberance for life back, and take your life to the next level—then *The Breakup Pivot* series *is* for you!

Our heart is something special and delicate. We protect it, cherish it and keep it so very close to us. But when we are in a relationship and feel safe and loved, we open ourselves up and give our heart to that other person as a representation of the deep caring and loving feelings we have for them.

Imagine this. We have inside of us a delicate glass heart that we keep in a little compartment lined with bubble wrap on all sides. When we fall in love, we take this heart out and hand it to the person to whom we want to show our feelings. The expectation is always that they will take excellent care of our heart. We trust that they won't drop it, break it, abandon it, or leave it unprotected for it to get scratched or chipped. Yet heartache is a direct result of that person not taking good care of our heart. It sucks. I know. We trust them to treat our heart the same way we would.

Very few of us in our lifetime escape the experience of heartbreak. Heartbreak, if you let it, can do one of two things: (1) derail you from your goals and purpose or (2) be a catalyst to do the painful work that results in getting you happy, healthy and whole.

Now is time to take your heart back from that person, buff out the scratches and dents, polish it up, kiss it, and put it back in its bubble-wrapped insulated box. This is called **HEALING**.

You are not alone, even though you may feel alone. For some of you, it may be your second, third, or fourth heartbreak, but the pain is just as real and deep as heartbreak number one.

Reading this book is the first step in being proactive in your healing. No matter how bad your situation may seem in this moment, one day it will be a distant memory.

Volume I: *Overcoming Heartbreak* covers six phases of breakup grief that you may experience over the ending of your relationship. Those phases are:

- 💔 Shock
- 💔 Denial
- 💔 Anger
- 💔 Depression
- 💔 Desperate for Answers and/or Contact
- 💔 Acceptance

These six phases are specific to the heartbreak grief experience but modeled after the Five Stages of Grief introduced by Dr. Elisabeth Kubler-Ross, a Swiss-American psychiatrist, in her best-selling book *On Death and Dying*. In her book, Kubler-Ross describes how terminally ill patients go through five stages of grief when faced with imminent death—denial, anger, bargaining, depression, and acceptance. Although Kubler-Ross called these *stages*, I see *stages* as being finite and not fluid. For example, you start with stage 1—and there is a beginning, middle, and end to the stage—and then you move into stage 2. This pattern continues through the five stages. However, I prefer to use phases, which are different. Phases are very fluid and flexible— they move in and out of one another. You may feel anger and flow into a depression and then flow back into anger or possibly back into denial.

Each chapter is uniquely structured into five sections:

MARIAH'S STORY. The first section will be *Mariah's Story*. You will follow the emotional post-heartbreak journey of a fictional character named Mariah to help identify certain patterns of behavior you may be experiencing.

IT'S IMPORTANT TO KNOW. The second section of each chapter will provide you with information to identify the phase you are in, as well as offer some tools and techniques to help you manage and get through the phase.

LET'S DO THE WORK. The third section will offer exercises or journal questions for you to work on self-discovery and development. It is important to not just read the contents of this book but to also put things into action. It will be challenging at times to get in touch with the pain, but you have to in order to heal and grow.

In addition to doing the exercises and answering the journal questions, I recommend keeping a separate journal to help you track your daily thoughts and emotions through this post-breakup period. Journaling can provide the following benefits:

- 💔 Clarity of thought and feelings.
- 💔 Reduction of stress. Writing about anger, sadness, and other painful emotions helps to release the intensity of these feelings.

AFFIRMATION. The fourth section will provide a positive affirmation. You do not have to say it in a mirror or hug yourself, but if you want to facilitate the healing process, you need to rewire your brain and train it to think differently. Affirmations are beneficial to healing because they:

💔 Motivate you to act.

💔 Change your negative thought patterns into positive ones.

💔 Influence your subconscious mind to access new beliefs.

💔 Help you feel positive about yourself and boost your self-confidence.

MOVIE TIME RECOMMENDATION. The last section provides a movie recommendation for that chapter phase. Movie therapy is considered an effective psychological tool for the following reasons:

💔 *Identification:* As we relate with characters in a movie it allows us to find hope through their story.

💔 *Learning:* Watching movies help us learn and become more creative.

💔 *Duration:* The length of a typical movie is almost the same as a therapy session.

💔 *Attention:* By focusing on the visuals and sounds, we tend to become more mindful and escape from our debilitating thoughts.

❦ *Relaxation:* Movies enable us to disconnect, revitalize and relax.

❦ *Enjoyment:* Through various fictional yet relatable scenarios, movies can make us laugh and improve our mental health.

❦ *Dealing with Loss:* Movies offer us new perspectives about life and help us in dealing with heartbreak by changing our attitude.

❦ *Cathartic Release:* Movies on breakups can help you face your deepest emotions—allowing you to shed your tears and experience relief.

This book was not written to be read once and put away. Each chapter is to be revisited as often as you need and to be used over the course of many months. It can be used in addition to and in conjunction with therapy or other support groups.

6 PHASES OF HEARTBREAK GRIEF

SHOCK

- A primal response to a traumatic loss
- Protects you from overwhelming emotions
- May feel like numbness or isolation from reality

DENIAL

- A state of disbelief
- Refusing to admit there is a problem
- You may avoid talking about the breakup

ANGER

- Can result from feelings of abandonment
- Upset at yourself, your Ex or another person you might blame for the breakup
- May spark a desire for revenge or retaliation to make him feel your pain

DESPERATE FOR ANSWERS AND/ OR CONTACT

- Struggling to find meaning for what has happened
- Desiring to tell your story
- Reaching out to your Ex by phone/text or stalking his social media

DEPRESSION

- Experiencing symptoms like sleep and appetite disturbance, intense sadness, loneliness and crying spells
- This phase can feel like it will last forever

ACCEPTANCE

- Comes with accepting the reality that the relationship is over
- You choose to move on with your life

5 FACTS ABOUT THE PHASES
OF HEARTBREAK GRIEF

Our grief is as individual as our lives. Each woman is unique in how she copes with feelings of Heartbreak Grief.

Not everyone will go through all of the 6 phases of Heartbreak Grief.

The 6 phases of Heartbreak Grief do not have a predictable, uniform and linear pattern.

You can switch back and forth between each of the 6 phases of Heartbreak Grief.

The 6 phases of Heartbreak Grief are simply tools to help us frame and identify what we are feeling.

THE BREAKUP PIVOT

Heartbreak Grief Overview

There Are Six Phases Of Heartbreak Grief

Everyone experiences loss and grief in their own unique way. There is no time frame for grief *or* an exact order. These six phases help us frame and identify what we may be feeling. Not everyone will go through *all* the phases *or* go through them in the same order.

As You Read This Book, Keep In Mind:

- 💔 You need to feel the pain to heal the pain.
- 💔 Your grief will probably hurt more before it hurts less.
- 💔 You will not always feel this bad.

These Are Some Emotions Associated With Heartbreak Grief:

(Yes, you are normal if you are feeling any of these…)

- 💔 Denial
- 💔 Sadness

- 💔 Anger
- 💔 Numbness
- 💔 Anxiety
- 💔 Loneliness
- 💔 Obsession (with memories of your ex)

These Are Some Physical Symptoms Associated With Heartbreak Grief:

(Yes, you are normal if you are experiencing any of these...)

- 💔 Difficulty with concentration
- 💔 Crying
- 💔 Confusion
- 💔 Social isolation
- 💔 Sleep changes (e.g. sleeping more or finding it hard to sleep)
- 💔 Anxiety attacks
- 💔 Appetite changes (e.g. decreased eating or comfort eating)

The Clarity Journal Exercise

In her book *Breaking Up and Bouncing Back*, Samantha Burns, LMHC, recommends a clarity journal exercise which is very helpful. In your journal, create five sections— each labeled with one of the phases of heartbreak grief: (a) Shock, (b) Denial, (c) Anger, (d) Desperate for Answers and/ or Contact, (e) Depression, and (f) Acceptance. As you go through the next days, weeks and months, use the space in your journal to write down your emotions, thoughts, actions, and experiences that fit into each category. THEN, after each experience, identify one concrete thing you can do to push through the phase that will move you toward the final phase of acceptance. For example:

<u>Shock</u>

December 14—I felt like I was hit by a Mack truck when he told me he wanted a divorce. All I could do was lie on the bed curled up in a fetal position for the next two hours. I feel like I am in an alternate universe.

A step that I can take to move out of shock:

♥ **Not isolate myself and call my sister to talk it out**.

<u>Denial</u>

December 19—Six months ago we had purchased tickets to see Hamilton at the Fox Theater in Atlanta. Even though we broke up, neither one of us was giving up our ticket to the sold-out show. He will be picking me up tonight so we can go in one car.

A step that I can take to move out of denial:

💔 **Get dressed up, be charming, enjoy the show, guard my heart, and remember the ugly and painful reason for the breakup.**

Anger

December 26 - I can't believe he had the nerve to ask me to split the cost of breaking the lease. He should pay since he was the one who ended the relationship!

A step that I can take to move me out of anger:

💔 **After work head straight to kick boxing class where I will pretend that I am punching him in his face.**

Desperate For Answers and/or Contact

January 20 - I caved in and texted him "I've been thinking about you. Hope all is well. Call me when you get a chance." He never responded. It is driving me crazy…Checking my text messages like a heroin addict. Why do I continue to do this to myself?

A step that I can take to move out of desperation:

❤ **Acknowledge that I am feeling lonely and senti-mental right now and call a trusted friend to talk it out.**

Depression

February 13 - I am completely deflated... crushed... overwhelmed with sadness. No matter what I do, I just cannot shake it. I feel borderline suicidal.

A step that I can take to move me out of depression:

❤ **Call my best friend, Gabby—she knows exactly what to say to make me feel better.**

Acceptance

November 2 - Today I realized that I am actually feeling excited for Thanksgiving, whereas last month I was sad about buying my ticket home because he wouldn't be coming with me.

A step that I can take to stay in acceptance:

❤ **Talk to my family about how I am feeling and tell them I appreciate their love and support while I am home celebrating the holiday.**

This is a big step. Allow yourself to be vulnerable. Feel the pain. Have the courage to heal and the strength to move on.

Heartbreak Grief Self-Assessment

Dealing with a breakup is both challenging and painful. Answering these questions will help you gain a better perspective of your situation and get through your heartbreak grieving process.

1. On a scale from 0-10, how is your breakup interfering with your daily life? (There is no right or wrong answer here.)

    0___1___2___3___4___5___6___7___8___9___**10**
    [What breakup?]   [can't get out of bed]

2. What do you think is the **main** reason you broke up?
    a. Fell out of love
    b. Distance/move
    c. Finances
    d. Infidelity
    e. Incompatible lifestyle
    f. Family
    g. Religion

h. Career

i. Fear of commitment

j. I have no idea

k. Other

3. The hardest part of the breakup is...... (Choose as many as apply to you.)

a. Losing the person

b. Managing financially

c. I cannot stop thinking about him

d. Losing future plans

e. Being single/dating again

f. Feeling lonely

g. Not knowing if his love was real

h. Not getting closure

i. Not knowing if I will find someone better

j. Not talking to him

k. Seeing him with someone else

l. Seeing him online/on social media

m. Seeing him in real life

n. Feeling depressed

o. Sleeping alone/eating alone

4. How long do you think it will take for you to move on from the breakup?

   a. A few weeks
   b. A few months
   c. Six months
   d. A year
   e. Years
   f. More than two years
   g. I will never move on
   h. I have already moved on

5. If you could ask your ex anything about your breakup and he was compelled to tell you the complete truth, what would you ask him?

_____

_____

_____

_____

_____

_____

6. What are some things that comfort you? How can you lessen your grief?

_____

_____

_____

_____

7. What could others do to assist you? Do you need someone to talk to? Watch the kids for a while? Run to the store for you? Whom can you reach out to for help with these tasks?

_____

_____

_____

_____

8. Do you need professional help in dealing with your heartbreak grief? Where can you find help in your community? What are some support groups that can help? Can you reach out to your faith community?

_____

_____

_____

_____

9. What could you choose to be happy about or thankful for in your life right now? Career? Faith community? Family members? Friends?

_____

_____

_____

_____

10. What are some activities you enjoy doing? What is one new hobby you have always wanted to try? What do you need to get started?

_____

_____

_____

_____

11. What is one valuable lesson that you learned from the relationship?

_____

_____

_____

_____

Prologue

Mariah Carson is a 33-year-old real estate agent who lives in Atlanta, Georgia. She has been dating Nick, a 41-year-old financial planner—who lives in an Atlanta suburb—for 20 months when they break up. Mariah has never been married before, but Nick has been twice divorced and has twin daughters that live with his last ex-wife in Florida.

Nick and Mariah's relationship begins when they meet on Tinder. For those that are not familiar with Tinder, it is one of the many online dating apps available that lets you "window shop" for a potential mate. Mariah and Nick have instant chemistry on the phone and a lot in common so Nick decides to ask Mariah out to dinner to meet in person. The first date is at a trendy restaurant in Atlanta that has great ambiance and even better food. Mariah is smitten on the first date. Nick is tall, well dressed and quite handsome. He has kind brown eyes and a killer smile. The vibe between them is easy and the conversation flows effortlessly. By mid-meal, Mariah notices that her cheeks hurt because she has been smiling so much. The date soon turns into a two-location date when Nick suggests they forgo dessert at the first spot to head over for coffee and dessert at Café Intermezzo—known for their decadent home-made Italian desserts. Mariah and Nick just clicked.... *verrry* well.

The following is a peek inside Mariah's relationship with Nick over the past 20 months.

Mariah's Pre-Story

Months 1-2: Nick heavily courts Mariah with his award-winning potato salad and lots of quality time—her primary love language. Envision it... a perfect romantic date at an exclusive winery in northern Georgia, Nick accompanies Mariah to her weekly Wednesday night Bible study that she refuses to give up, outdoor music concerts, many date nights at restaurants that cater to their vegan lifestyle, hiking on the nature trails at Stone Mountain Park, and a weekend trip to Washington, DC, where Nick shows Mariah his "old stomping ground."

Month 3: Nick presents Mariah with a sparkling pink key to his apartment in the suburbs of Atlanta. Things feel like they are moving a bit fast to Mariah, but she thinks the gesture is super sweet and she accepts it. Slowly she is letting her emotional guard down. She is unlocking her heart.

Month 4: This is a memorable month…Nick's birthday and the first time they "make the magic happen." It is also their first international trip together—five days in sunny Jamaica. Mariah and Nick both feel like they are on their honeymoon. Nothing but love, love, and more love. They both cannot believe how fortunate they are to have found each other. She is unlocking the box and handing Nick her heart.

Month 5: Nick invites Mariah to tag along on his routine parental visit to Jacksonville, Florida, to meet his 10-year-old twin daughters, Tracey and Stacey. His daughters, from his previous marriage, live with their mother and Nick visits them twice a month.

Month 6: Mariah is spending more time at Nick's apartment than her own place. Nick clears out space in his closet and in the bathroom for Mariah. Things are feeling very comfortable.

Month 7: Mariah and Nick talk about marriage and getting matching tattoos. It would be the first tattoo for both of them.

Month 8: Nick takes a solo trip to meet with Mariah's parents in Maryland to ask for permission to marry Mariah and gets her father's blessing. Nick buys an engagement ring.

Month 9: Nick proposes to Mariah in front of friends and family on her birthday and surprises her with a beautiful diamond ring. Mariah happily and tearfully accepts his proposal.

Month 10: Nick's apartment lease is almost up. Mariah and Nick discuss and agree to move into a beautiful rental home together in the suburbs of Atlanta since they will be married soon. Mariah envisions where the Christmas tree will be and her happy future with Nick in this house.

Month 11: Mariah and Nick start pre-marital counseling at Mariah's home church. There is a family trip with Mariah's parents to West Palm Beach, Florida for the Thanksgiving holiday. Mariah and Nick start looking for a wedding venue to have a small and intimate wedding in the summer of the following year.

Month 12: Mariah and Nick visit his extended family in Chicago, Illinois, for the Christmas holiday. It is also on this trip that Mariah meets two of Nick's high school friends and their wives. At the dinner table there is a discussion about coordinating a friends' reunion trip with five couples for upcoming May. Nick verbally commits himself and Mariah for the St. Lucia trip. This raises an eyebrow for Mariah because she and Nick have not even finalized wedding plans or discussed where their honeymoon will be. Mariah ignores the "yellow flag" and just goes with the flow.

Month 13: Mariah begins wedding dress shopping. This is also the month she starts her Weight Watchers program to lose 20 pounds.

Month 14: Mariah plans a romantic Valentine's Day with Nick. However, she starts to really notice that the kisses are not what they used to be. In the past, Nick would almost "inhale" Mariah and exude this little moan when he kissed her. He is seemingly not as "present" nor as intense as he once was.

Month 15: Mariah surprises Nick with a trip to Las Vegas, Nevada with Nick's two sisters and their spouses. Mariah bonds with Alexis, Nick's youngest sister, as they start developing a friendship. However, Mariah is feeling a slight disconnect with Nick on this trip. Nick is spending more time with his brothers-in-law than with Mariah. He is not as attentive or patient with her. He is quick to leave her in the hotel room before she is finished with her hair and makeup to meet up with his family, whereas before, Nick would never let Mariah out of his sight.

Month 16: Nick goes to "Happy Hour" after work with Ron, one of his co-workers, and does not call Mariah to let her know he will be coming home late. This is totally out of character for Nick. He would always stay in communication with Mariah throughout the day and if he were to make a stop after work, he would let Mariah know—and vice versa.

Month 17: Nick's birthday month. Mariah and Nick fly to romantic St. Lucia for the friends' reunion trip. However, all Nick is interested in doing is lying by the pool and working on his tan. Mariah senses the lack of doting attention but chalks it up to the relationship "settling in."

Month 18: Mariah goes to Maryland to visit her father for Father's Day. Nick stays home in Georgia. Mariah begins to have problems reaching Nick on the phone. When they talk, he seems a bit detached and cold. When Mariah addresses it with Nick, he says that she is acting very insecure and he doesn't know why. Yup! Nick went there. The ole classic "turn the table on you" game. Mariah comes to the realization that Nick has totally stopped bringing up the wedding plans and her "she-tuition" (that female intuition that we all have) kicks into overdrive.

Month 19: Mariah sinks to an all-time low and out of desperation for answers, she checks Nick's phone and finds text messages between him and another woman—Denise. Nick is saying he had a great time at her birthday party and that he finds her sexy. **What..the... what?????** Mariah hurriedly takes pictures of the text messages. Later when she has some privacy, Mariah figures out that the timeframe of this party was the weekend she was in Maryland visiting her father for Father's Day! Something Nick failed to mention he had on his calendar during one of Mariah's very "insecure" phone calls to him that weekend. Mariah takes a few days to process all this new information. She decides not to say anything yet and maintains the status quo.

Month 20: Well, you know the saying "Don't ask a question that you don't want the answer to"—Mariah asks and gets the answer that she does not want to hear.

Join Mariah on the next part of her journey from devastating heartbreak to her living her best life, filled with joy, purpose, gratitude and influence. By doing the work and using the tools and techniques in the upcoming chapters, it is my hope that you too find peace, joy, and a new and improved version of YOU.

Chapter 1

SHOCK

- A primal response to a traumatic loss
- Protects you from overwhelming emotions
- May feel like numbness or isolation from reality

Shock *is defined as a sudden upsetting or surprising event or experience.*

(The Oxford Dictionary)

Mariah's Story

Mariah has been struggling to find the 'perfect' time to have a sensitive conversation with Nick. *That* moment finally comes tonight, right after they finish eating dinner. All the thoughts come rushing to Mariah at once causing her heart to beat a mile a minute. She knows she just needs to start the conversation, as she puts her hand on his upper thigh.

MARIAH: "Honey Bun, you know that I love you, right?" Mariah calls Nick by his pet name to soften the deadly blow that she is about to deliver.

NICK: "I love you too," Nick replies with his eyes locked on the television in the family room.

MARIAH: "Well…I was wondering who *Denise* is and why you went to her birthday party last month and never told me."

NICK: "Who?" Nick replies with a puzzled and defiant look.

MARIAH: "DEE….NISE??" Mariah says firmly.

NICK: "What are you are talking about?"

Now Mariah was hoping it would not come to her having to whip out the physical evidence, but Nick is steadily playing her for a fool. With her phone only inches away from her on the table, she unlocks it and goes straight to her photo gallery.

MARIAH: "Does this bring back your memory?" Mariah says as she holds the phone in front of his face to display a screenshot of text messages between him and Denise.

NICK: "Damn. *Why* were you snooping on my phone!!??"

MARIAH: "Yup. Damn is right! And *don't* try to change the subject!!"

Nick is quiet for a moment as he processes the ambush and tries to gather his thoughts. However, Mariah quickly chimes back in wanting to know answers. She is ready to get clarity on what is exactly going on in her relationship with Nick.

MARIAH: "What's going on, Nick? I thought we were a team. But honestly, I feel like you changed the playbook and didn't bother to tell me. You got me on the playing field and **your** butt is sitting on the bench!"

NICK:	"Look, I'm sorry. I don't know what else to say."
MARIAH:	Mariah pauses before the question she really wants to ask. "Do you still want to marry me?"
NICK:	With an airy sigh, Nick shakes his head and says, "No."

Mariah is devastated and instantly feels nauseated. All sense of reality at this point seems detached. The next few days in the house with Nick are a roller coaster of emotions for Mariah. For the most part she is sad with a touch of anger and is in constant "processing mode." She and Nick talk about and agree not to renew the lease for the house that terminates in two months. And, only as Mariah can handle it, they talk more in depth about the 'WHY?'— why Nick does not want to get married.

It's Important To Know

The Shock Phase. Shock is like anesthesia that keeps us from having to face a difficult situation all at once. It is a temporary escape from reality. This shock phase may last anywhere from a few minutes to a few hours to a few days. If it goes on for some weeks, it probably is unhealthy grief and professional help needs to be sought.

What Psychological Shock Is. According to Psychology Today, psychological shock is when you experience a surge of strong emotions and a corresponding physical reaction, in response to a (typically unexpected) stressful event, like a relationship breakup.

Symptoms of Psychological Shock:

- 💔 The main and most common symptom of shock is feeling a surge of adrenaline.
- 💔 You may also feel jittery or physically sick, like you are going to vomit or have diarrhea.
- 💔 Your mind will likely feel very foggy, or like you cannot think straight.
- 💔 You may feel out of your body.
- 💔 Your chest may feel tight.
- 💔 You may feel a disconnection from what is happening, like you're watching a movie of events unfolding rather than actually being there.
- 💔 You may feel like you want to run.

Timeline. Everyone has their own unique timeline for getting over shock. Some people recover from emotional shock in several hours. Others take several days, or several weeks. And for some, depending on what they go through, shock can even go on for six weeks or more.

You May Experience 'Delayed' Emotional Shock.

You might think an event has not upset you, only to feel symptoms of emotional shock days or weeks later.

Acute Stress Disorder. Are you in an absolute rage over someone taking your parking spot or crying just because you burned your toast? It is possible that you have developed acute stress disorder (ASD).

According to PsychCentral.com, acute stress disorder is characterized by the development of severe anxiety, dissociation, and other symptoms that occurs within one month after exposure to an extreme traumatic stressor. As it relates to your breakup, you may experience difficulty concentrating, irritable mood, feel detached from your body, experience the world as unreal or dreamlike or have increasing difficulty recalling specific details about the breakup. This must last for a minimum of three (3) days and a maximum of four (4) weeks and must occur within four (4) weeks of the traumatic event.

Let's Do The Work

Journal Questions

1. Mariah's shocking moment was when Nick let her know he no longer wanted to marry her. What was/were your shocking moment(s)?

_____

_____

_____

_____

2. What parts of Mariah's story can you relate to?

_____

_____

_____

_____

3. What emotions are you feeling now?

_____

_____

_____

_____

Affirmation

"I am worthy of love even when my heart is hurting."

Movie Time Recommendation

Sex and The City – The Movie
(2008) *2h 25min* Rated R
Comedy/Drama/Romance

Spoiler Alert
The synopsis below may give away important plot points.

Carrie Bradshaw (Sarah Jessica Parker) finally gets the commitment she has dreamed of from the non-committal Mr. Big (Chris Noth). They are getting married. Having been married before, he would prefer a small affair. But Carrie soon gets carried away with dreams of a fashionista's dream wedding as she tries on wedding dresses from top designers. Mr. Big gets cold feet after talking to Miranda (Cynthia

Nixon), who is really projecting the problems she is facing in her own marriage with Steve (David Eigenberg). Things have dwindled for Steve and Miranda, leading him to have an affair. They separate as a result.

When Mr. Big deserts Carrie at the altar, the girls take off on what would have been her honeymoon in Mexico. The girls have a great time, but it takes Carrie a while before she can laugh again. Samantha (Kim Cattrall) calls Miranda out on letting herself go, suggesting that she has been neglecting herself and her marriage. Charlotte (Kristen Davis) is paranoid about drinking the water, but inadvertently drinks some in the shower. Unfortunately, this leads to an embarrassing case of diarrhea. Samantha has been finding it frustrating being so far away from her boyfriend, Smith (Jason Lewis), whose acting career has taken off.

On her return, Carrie decides to get her life in order by hiring an assistant named Louise (Jennifer Hudson)— who it turns out is also having relationship troubles. However, things turn around for Louise when her childhood sweetheart proposes. She ends up leaving her employment with Carrie.

On Valentine's Day, Miranda confesses to Carrie that it was her fault that Mr. Big got cold feet. But it ends up that Carrie and Mr. Big reconcile and have a small wedding at the courthouse.

Chapter 2

DENIAL

- A state of disbelief
- Refusing to admit there is a problem
- You may avoid talking about the breakup

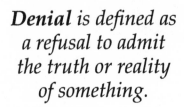

Denial *is defined as*
a refusal to admit
the truth or reality
of something.

(Merriam-Webster Dictionary)

Mariah's Story

Mariah still loves Nick. She is also still having sex with Nick even though her world is crashing all around her. What she is unable to process is that the future she visualized so clearly with Nick is **not** going to happen. No wedding, no marriage, no children, no growing old together and no more routine...with Nick. Mariah feels like something is truly dying inside of her.

Because of Mariah's controlling nature, she decides in her mind that she and Nick will remain in a monogamous relationship and just take marriage off the table... for now. The problem with her plan is that Nick was not privy to that conversation in her head and he has already been emotionally divesting from the relationship by "friending" and chatting with more women on Facebook.

Their lack of the meeting of the minds on this issue plays out in the following conversation between Nick and Mariah in the master bathroom while they are brushing their teeth and getting ready for bed.

NICK: "Um, I bought some extra packing boxes from Home Depot if you need some," Nick says dryly to Mariah.

This somehow is an emotional sting to Mariah—in her mind she is thinking, 'Dang, Nick is really serious about this moving thing. He's gotten boxes *already*!!' But she plays it cool.

MARIAH: "Thank you," Mariah replies equally as dry. "You know, I've been thinking."

NICK: Nick braces himself and takes a deep breath. "About what?"

MARIAH: "We need to pray, Nick."

NICK: "About what?"

MARIAH: "…About us!! We need to pray about us and our relationship! God can help us get back on track."

Mariah immediately stops talking as she sees Nick's expression in the bathroom mirror and realizes Nick is dead serious about his desire not to pray.

MARIAH: "Look, Nick, I'm not here to *force* you to pray for us…If you don't want to pray… then…"

Mariah tapers off her sentence as she takes her contact lenses out.

In Nick's mind, he and Mariah have come to an understanding that the relationship is not going to progress to marriage. Which means there is no going backwards from fiancé to just boyfriend and girlfriend and it is time to move on. But Mariah did not get that memo. *Or* she did get the memo but is just in denial— hanging on to hope that things will not drastically change between them.

As the weeks progress, life is different now. Where there once was a joyful energy in the house, everything now seems to be deflated, quiet and sad. Both Mariah and Nick are emotionally divesting. Neither is saying "I love you" anymore, which used to be a staple in their vocabulary. But more noticeably, Mariah has stopped calling Nick by his pet name, Honey Bun, and now just calls him Nick. Yes, the tide is changing but Mariah holds out the hope that she and Nick will still be together in a monogamous relationship—just not getting married.

Oh yeah, Mariah also has yet to tell her parents. They call the house and still chat Nick up like he is their third son. It is nothing but a love fest between all of them and that makes Mariah feel good. Deep down she hopes that this is just a phase that she and Nick are going through, and it will all work out in the end.

NICK: "Your parents called while you were at the grocery store. When are you going to tell them that we called the wedding off?"

MARIAH: "I will. I will. I just haven't found the right time." Mariah pauses and puts her hand on Nick's shoulder to delicately and tentatively ask, "Nick, what was it that I did that made you change your mind about marriage?"

NICK: "You didn't do anything wrong, Mariah. Please don't feel like that."

MARIAH: "Then…why did you stop loving me?"

NICK: "I still have love for you. But like I told you before, I've been married twice before and I realized that I'm just not ready to get married again. I'm still recovering financially from my last ex-wife."

Nick's answer just does not make sense to Mariah. Why get this far down the road to say you don't want to continue? Mariah senses it is something deeper. She starts to replay the entire relationship back in her head— frame by frame. Did she complain too much? Was she not fulfilling him sexually? Was she spending too much money and he got nervous and afraid? ***What was it***??

To help deal with the pain, Mariah turns to her favorite wine and calls her college friend, Gabrielle. Gabrielle, who Mariah affectionately calls Gabby, lives in Houston, Texas, with her husband of eight years, Duane, and their three children.

MARIAH: "Hey girl. I have something to tell you," Mariah says deeply and heavily.

GABBY: "Uh-oh. I can hear it in your voice. What's going on?"

MARIAH: "The wedding is off. Nick changed his mind about getting married."

GABBY: "What!!? Why?" Gabby pauses. "I'm so sorry, Sis. Are you all right?"

MARIAH: "He...he just checked out. I found some inappropriate text messages. I questioned him about them, and he said he's not ready to get married again. I am still processing it." Mariah begins to well up with tears. "I gave him everything, Gabby. My mind, body, and soul because I thought he was the One. My soul mate and life mate."

GABBY: "Are you still living together?"

MARIAH:	"We're in the same house until our lease is up in another two months."
GABBY:	"How is that working out?"
MARIAH:	"It's weird and an emotional roller coaster, to say the least. We still sleep in the same bed. I really do still love him. I know I sound crazy but I still want to spend the rest of my life with him."
GABBY:	"Are you still having sex with Nick??"
MARIAH:	Sheepishly, "Yeah…but…"
GABBY:	"Sis, you are making it harder on yourself by still having sex with Nick. You know that, right?"
MARIAH:	"I know…but I keep hoping that he will have this miraculous revelation and truly see what a great catch I am and that no one will love him as much as I do. Plus, I'm not ready yet to give up the sex." Mariah pauses. "But honestly, Gabby, I saw some yellow flags along the way. I just didn't want to look too closely."
GABBY:	"What flags are you talking about?"
MARIAH:	"Signs that were telling me his feelings were changing. You know that song that asks 'How do you know if he loves you so?

It's in his kiss'? Well, one sign was that Nick's kisses had changed. They became more hurried. Less passionate…more routine. We lost that deep intimate connection somewhere along the way."

GABBY: "Hmmmmm."

MARIAH: "Another sign was that Nick started making big decisions without consulting with me… like committing to the all-inclusive friends' trip to St. Lucia earlier this year."

GABBY: "You went with him, though, right?"

MARIAH: "Yeah, but, one—we were not balling like that and two—we had not even decided on a wedding venue or where we were going on our honeymoon. Then, I started noticing Nick had stopped talking about our wedding plans altogether. Bottom line…I was afraid to have that conversation with Nick because I did not want to rock the boat."

GABBY: "So you felt that things were off?"

MARIAH: "I guess my gut knew something, but it was the lack of eye contact that really made me take notice."

GABBY: "What do you mean?"

MARIAH: "Nick stopped looking me in the eyes when we would talk to each other. Either he looked at the television, or any other place but in my eyes. When I mentioned it to him, he just put it back on me that I wanted to complain about something."

GABBY: "He's an ass. I'm sorry, Mariah, I have to say it. I want you to know how beautiful and amazing you are! I want to remind you that you are stronger than you think, and I am here for you to help you get through this."

It's Important To Know

The Denial Phase. Even though you may come out of the initial shock, you will most likely experience times in the succeeding days and months when the reality of the loss of the relationship comes over you again. You will say, "I can't believe it's over. I'm just not there emotionally yet." As you proceed, all the feelings you were denying begin to surface and you start to feel the pain.

The Pain is Real. It is not your imagination. Brain studies show that **love is an addiction**. That is, the brain reacts extremely similarly to the loss of love as it does to withdrawal from a drug. Intense cravings, separation anxiety, obsessive thoughts, physical and emotional dependency, reality distortion, and a loss of self-control are all signs of withdrawal from both substances and love.

Dr. Guy Winch, a licensed psychologist and author, teaches that as we experience withdrawal of romantic love, our unconscious mind chooses our memories of the ex as a form of methadone to ease the process. This is the reason we keep going down one rabbit hole after another, even when we know it is going to make us feel worse. Our instincts tell us that we are trying to solve a mystery, but what we are doing is seeking our next fix. This is what makes heartbreak difficult to heal. Addicts know they are addicted. But heartbroken people do not. You have to recognize that with every trip down memory lane, every text you send, every second you stalk his social media, you just feed your addiction, deepening your emotional pain and complicating your recovery.

We Have to Feel the Pain in Order to Heal. We must feel it to heal it —if we do not, our bodies will stay in a place of *dis*-ease which will eventually lead to disease in the body.

Crying is Carthartic. Crying is healthy and facilitates the healing. You may feel yourself wanting to cry at unexpected times or places. If you need to, excuse yourself and retreat somewhere private. However, if you feel safe and in a supportive environment, go ahead and cry openly and honestly, unashamed of your tears.

There is a Difference Between Being Cordial with the Ex and Staying Friends with the Ex. Being cordial means friendly and staying friends entails a deeper involvement in each other's lives. Staying friends with the ex could be very weird. You are in a different space now and the boundaries have definitely changed. You are not having intimate dinners or sharing deeply personal things about your life anymore. Many things will be off limits now which will result in painfully awkward 'small talk' and the friendship will ultimately prove to be unsatisfying. Contrary to your belief, this will just add to your pain instead of easing the pain. In the end, you will delay getting on with your life and getting whole.

If You Can, Change Your Environment. Get away to a new destination. Go visit friends or family in another state or country. If you like the beach, go to the beach and connect with nature. It can be for a short trip or several weeks.

Don't Romanticize the Relationship. We tend to want to only remember the good and romantic parts and forget the parts that hurt our feelings or disrespected us or embarrassed us. Write down a list of all the annoying and disrespectful and toxic things about your ex. Review the list as needed.

Don't Rush into Another Relationship. You may have a strong desire to numb the pain by jumping into the arms of another man for emotional and physical companionship. DON'T!! It ends up not being fair to the new person or to yourself. This journey is about healing and becoming the best version of yourself— becoming happy, whole, and prosperous! If you rush into a new relationship too soon you are delaying your healing process. It is like putting a Band-Aid over a deep wound when you need to go to the doctor and get stitches and heal the correct way.

You May Want to Turn to Alchohol or Drugs to Numb the Pain. Avoid doing this. Alcohol and drugs may feel good temporarily, but all they do is mask the problem with no solution. You want to have a clear view of your situation and mind-altering substances distort reality. Seek out counseling and healthy alternatives like exercise and/or a healthy hobby.

You May Feel Rejected. Your self-esteem has taken a major hit. You may be wondering what the other women have that you don't have. And you keep asking yourself:

- 💔 Why wasn't I good enough for him to want to stay in the relationship with me?
- 💔 What went wrong? Why did he change his mind? What did I do?

You May Pass Up New Opportunites. Dr. Gary Brown, a prominent relationship therapist in Los Angeles, explains in an article by Elite Daily, that another sign of denial is when you give up opportunities and put your life on hold in order to remain available just in case your ex wants to get back together. For example, if "you are offered a new and exciting job in a new city that you would love to be in and that will absolutely be a career enhancement — and you turn this opportunity down because you are still in denial that the breakup is not real or permanent," Dr. Brown says that's a major red flag that you are in a serious state of denial.

Let's Do The Work

Empty Chair Exercise

The Empty Chair exercise is a key technique used in Gestalt therapy, developed by Fritz Perls—a notable German-born psychiatrist, that has been widely used by therapists since its inception in the 1940s. This talk therapy exercise lets you express your thoughts and feelings as if you were talking to a specific person—in this case, it will be your ex. Even though he is not present, you will direct your words and gestures at an empty chair and imagine him sitting in it while you talk.

First, create a peaceful space for your "meeting" with your ex. Next, place an empty chair facing you. Then "invite" your ex to join you. Imagine him in the empty chair. Imagine what he is wearing, what he smells like, and the expression on his face.

💔 Tell your ex about your unresolved feelings. (You can have your feelings written down beforehand or just speak off the cuff.) This includes any feelings such as pain, anger, resentment, guilt, hurt, rage, unexpressed love, disappointment, or fear. Tell him what he did or did not do that hurt you. Tell him how you felt about it. Try to avoid blaming statements, and speak instead in the "first person" about your own feelings and experience.

♥ For example, "I remember when…" "I was humiliated when…" "My heart was broken when…"

💔 Tell your ex how his behavior has emotionally, behaviorally, and possibly physically affected you. Tell him what your expectations were for how you wanted him to behave and how you wanted him to relate to you. Express everything you wish to say and ask at this time to get closure.

💔 Then, stand up and sit in the chair across from you, embodying your ex and responding to yourself as though you were him. Receive what you (as you ex) have just been told. Let it in. Reflect on the facts and the feelings that you heard yourself express. However, rather than answering with what you think your ex would say, ***respond with what you want to hear that will bring you closure***. Imagine how it feels for your ex to say these things *to you* and imagine the healing it brings you.

♥ For example, you may need to hear him say that he truly loved you and you raised the bar to an almost impossible standard for every person after you to be measured by. Or, that the relationship was special to him and even though it did not work out, you did nothing wrong.

💔 Write about your experience in your journal.

Journal Questions

1. In Mariah's conversation with Nick, she asked him what she did to make him change his mind about marriage. Do you blame yourself for the breakup? If so, why?

_____

_____

_____

_____

2. Based on what you read in this Chapter, are you in denial? List what actions you have been doing or not been doing that may be examples of your own denial.

_____

_____

_____

_____

3. Are you feeling sad? If yes, why are you sad?

_____

_____

_____

_____

Affirmation to Recite

"This breakup is the beginning of a positive new direction in my life."

Movie Time Recommendation

Silver Linings Playbook
(2012) *2h 2min* Rated R
Comedy/Drama/Romance

Spoiler Alert
The synopsis below may give away important plot points.

Life doesn't always go according to plan. Pat Solitano (Bradley Cooper) has lost everything—his house, his job, and is wife—after beating up his wife's lover and being sent to a mental hospital where he is diagnosed with bipolar disorder. He gets released to go live with his parents, but he is reluctant to take his medication or go to mandated therapy. The only thing he wants is to try to get back together with his wife, but she has written him off and taken out a restraining order against him. In his efforts to find his wife, Pat meets Tiffany (Jennifer Lawrence), who offers to help him in exchange for Pat being her ballroom dance partner. As their deal plays out, an unexpected bond begins to form between them, and silver linings appear in both of their lives.

THE BREAKUP PIVOT

Chapter 3

ANGER

- Can result from feelings of abandonment
- Upset at yourself, your Ex or another person you might blame for the breakup
- May spark a desire for revenge or retaliation to make him feel your pain

***Anger** is defined as
a strong feeling
of annoyance,
displeasure,
or hostility.*

(The Oxford Dictionary)

Mariah's Story

As Mariah unpacks the moving boxes in her new apartment, she is on autopilot. Slicing and opening. Slicing and opening. But she pauses at this next box. Mariah realizes this is the box packed with the photo albums and picture frames—memories that she and Nick had shared. As soon as Mariah plops down on the carpet in the middle of the living room, her cell phone rings. It is Mariah's older sister, Whitney, on FaceTime to check on her baby sister. Whitney lives in New Jersey and is on her fourth husband, Rob. If anyone is qualified to give advice on heartbreak—it's Whitney!

WHITNEY   "Hey, Bunny, I am calling to check on you." Bunny is Mariah's childhood family nickname. "You know that Mom, Dad and I are all concerned about you."

MARIAH: "Yeah, I know. I've been unpacking all day and feeling a bit overwhelmed. Right before you called, I came across pictures of me and Nick. I can't bear to look at them. It hurts too much."

WHITNEY: "It will get easier."

53

MARIAH: "When? *When*?" Mariah exasperates. "I just want to feel joy again."

WHITNEY: "You will. This too shall pass."

MARIAH: "I made a run to Costco yesterday. Nick and I would always do our weekly shopping together on Saturday or Sunday at Costco."

WHITNEY: "I love Costco," Whitney gleefully chimes in.

MARIAH: "Yeah—well, I *used* to love Costco. I can't even begin to describe the deluge of sadness and the floodgates of emotions I had in the store. I was literally crying as I pushed the cart down the frozen food aisle in search of some frozen hash browns." Mariah continues, "I'm an emotional wreck. I cry myself to sleep clutching my pillow. I have no appetite. I am sad. I cannot listen to the radio—the love songs are *killing* me. I am lonely. I am angry."

WHITNEY: "It's normal to feel that way. I think it is healthy to cry. But I want you to do two things. When you find yourself drifting into thoughts of Nick, switch your thought to something that makes you happy or smile. Like think of the fun time we had white water rafting for my 30th birthday or thoughts of lying on the beach listening to the waves crashing."

MARIAH: "Yeah, I can do that."

WHITNEY: "I also want you to only allow yourself to cry **no more** than an hour a day over Nick and the situation. Set aside this time at night. You will find out that you will need less and less time to cry as time goes on."

MARIAH: "I am just sad, Mariah. I miss him so much. Why did he do this to me? I trusted him and he abused my freaking heart! He basically lied to me and made me look like a fool."

WHITNEY: "It won't always be like this. When you find yourself starting to lose it during work hours or anytime that is not conducive to busting out in tears—remind yourself that you have a dedicated hour later that night to let the feelings flow. Put it on the shelf for later," Whitney advises.

MARIAH: "I'm feeling a bit overwhelmed. I'm still unpacking and I have a **lot** to do at work. If I had the flu or needed an operation, my job would allow me to take sick time to get better, but no one gives time off to nurse a broken heart."

WHITNEY: "I want you to consider seeing someone."

MARIAH: "I am far from ready to start dating again."

WHITNEY: "No, Bunny. I am talking about seeing a therapist. You need support through this process. Counseling helped me tremendously after my third divorce. Hopefully, you can get clarity on some issues and learn coping techniques so your emotions won't be all over the place."

MARIAH: "That's a good idea. I used to see Dr. Anderson a while back for my anxiety issues. I found her through my company's EAP-Employee Assistance Program-where I can get free counseling sessions. I will look into setting something up next week."

Mariah realizes that she has not had a moment to reach out to Gwen, who is married to Dan—Nick's co-worker and football buddy. Both couples spent many Sundays together watching football—alternating between the two homes. Mariah considers Gwen a close friend with whom she shares a love for baking and scrapbooking. She scrolls through her phone contacts and gives Gwen a call.

MARIAH: "Hi Gwen! I've been M.I.A.—so sorry."

GWEN: "Oh, no worries, girl. I know you have a lot going on. How are you doing?"

MARIAH: "I still can't believe that Nick did this to me. He really hurt me to my core. Do you think Dan knew of Nick's change of heart? Did he ever mention anything to you?"

GWEN: Being taking a bit off-guard, Gwen responds, "No...not that I can recall. Dan and Nick are guys, Mariah. They don't sit around sipping tea and talking about their feelings like us women do."

MARIAH: "You're right. It's that Nick just abandoned ship and I am left holding all of the emotional baggage. Men move on—seemingly like they don't have a care in the world."

GWEN: "Mariah, come on, I know for a fact that Nick loved you deeply. I'm sure his intent was not to hurt you, but it was either a little pinch now or deeper and more complicated hurt down the road."

MARIAH: "My mind gets that, but my heart...Damn my heart!"

It's Important To Know

"If you spend your time hoping someone will suffer the consequences for what they did to your heart, then you're allowing them to hurt you a second time in your mind."
Shannon L. Alder

What Anger Is. Anger is a basic human emotion that is experienced by all people. Anger is that unpleasant feeling that occurs when we think we have been injured, mistreated, or when we are faced with obstacles that keep us from attaining our personal goals. Anger is a necessary phase of the healing process. Be willing to feel your anger, even though it may seem endless.

Symptoms of Anger. All of us have experienced symptoms of anger—physical and mental signs—that tell us we are angry.

PHYSICAL SIGNS	MENTAL SIGNS	OTHER SIGNS
Fast heartbeat	Problems	Yelling
Sweating	concentrating	Swearing
Shaking	Confusion	Withdrawing from
Clenched jaws	Memory problems	others
Clenched fists	Thoughts of doing	Throwing things
Fast breathing	harm	Pacing
Headaches	Angry thoughts	
Stomach aches	Irritability	
Tight chest	Short tempered	
Tense muscles		
Frowning, scowling		
Red face		

Breathe and Count to Ten. When you feel yourself getting angry, take a long, deep inhalation, and as you do, say the number one to yourself. Then relax your entire body as you breathe out. Repeat the same process with the number two, all the way through at least ten, depending on how angry you are. As a result, you will be clearing your mind with a short meditation exercise. This will also help you de-stress and relax.

Take 5

Focus on:

5 things you can SEE

4 things you can HEAR

3 things you can FEEL

2 things you can TASTE

1 thing you can SMELL

You May Feel Anger Toward The Ex. Anger can be displayed in many ways. Some women go "Angela Bassett-Waiting to Exhale" angry on the ex. For those who have not seen that movie, I am referring to the scene in the movie where the main character (played by Angela Bassett) burns all of her cheating husband's clothes inside his car in front of their home, triggering the fire department and the police. It is not recommended to destroy property of your ex. That could cause more problems and possibly land you a night in jail. Not a good idea.

You May Feel Anger Toward Yourself. Stop the negative self-talk. Don't let your breakup tear down your self-esteem and make you feel like you are a failure or not worthy of love.

- 💔 Stop it. You cannot be responsible for someone else's actions.
- 💔 It is not you, it really is THEM.
- 💔 Anger for not heeding the red flags.
- 💔 Anger for staying longer than you should have.
- 💔 Overcoming that "It didn't work out AGAIN" anger.

You May Feel Anger Toward Mutual Friends That Take The Side of Your Ex. When a marriage or romantic relationship ends, it may result in "collateral damage" within intersecting friendscapes. This can be especially difficult when the breakup with a partner leads to the loss of mutual friends that were cherished as companions and confidantes. When romantic relationships fall apart, one of our first instincts is to find a sympathetic ear. When a former confidante now shows allegiance to the ex, it can feel like a double dose of betrayal. You may be angry at the ex whose behavior led to the breakup—**and** sad and confused that another friend sided with your ex over you.

Listen to Soothing Music. Now is not the time for heavy metal or the theme from Rocky. *Find something that soothes your emotions and listen for 15 minutes.* Experiment with different types of music until you find the best choice for you.

Pray. Praying can help calm you and release your anger. It may be rough right now, but God will see you through it, even if you feel alone. When anger and chaos start to kick in, simply whisper God's name and that simple act of faith will bring God closer to you, helping you to get your mind back on the right track. Always be thankful and count your blessings.

Find Healthy Ways to Express Your Anger

- 💔 Kickboxing class
- 💔 Axe throwing
- 💔 Karate class
- 💔 Talking to a therapist
- 💔 Journaling
- 💔 Exercise (e.g., join and go to a gym, walk around the block or to the market, or climb stairs in your building)

Don't Be Afraid to Get Help. Get professional help for serious anger issues. If you are regularly angry and cannot control your anger, seek out the help of a professional.

FINDING AN AFFORDABLE THERAPIST		
CHECK YOUR HEALTH INSURANCE.	**TRY UNIVERSITY COUNSELING CENTERS.**	**CALL AND ASK.**
Many insurance carriers cover mental health services (although there may be a cap on how many sessions are covered). Call them to get a list of "in-network" therapists in your area.	If your local university offers a psychology program, there is a good chance they offer a sliding-scale fee structure--a price based on your ability to pay.	There are many in private practice that do a few hours a week of pro bono work or therapy with clients who can afford to pay only a small fee. It does not hurt to call and ask.

Let's Do The Work

Journal Exercise:

1. Are you still angry? If so, what makes you angry?

_____

_____

_____

_____

2. What are two exercises or activities that you can start doing immediately to help diffuse your anger?

_____

_____

_____

_____

3. What are the advantages of letting go of your anger?

_____

_____

_____

_____

4. What would change in your life if you could be free of negative emotions?

_____

_____

_____

_____

5. Write down three blessings before going to bed tonight. What does each blessing mean to you?

_____

_____

_____

_____

Affirmation to Recite

"I choose to release anger, hurt, and negative self-talk."

Movie Time Recommendation

Waiting to Exhale

(1995) *2h 4min* Rated R

Comedy/Drama/Romance

Spoiler Alert

The synopsis below may give away important plot points.

Navigating through careers, family and romance, four friends bond over the shortcomings in their love lives –namely, the scarcity of good men. Both as the "other woman", Savannah (Whitney Houston) and Robin (Lela Rochon) carry on relationships with married men, each believing their lovers will leave their wives for them. On the flip side, Bernadine (Angela Bassett) ends up alone when her husband divorces her for his mistress. Meanwhile, Gloria (Loretta Devine) finds love with a new neighbor.

Chapter 4

DESPERATE FOR ANSWERS AND/OR CONTACT

- Struggling to find meaning for what has happened
- Desiring to tell your story
- Reaching out to your Ex by phone/text or stalking his social media

Desperate *is defined*
as having
an urgent need
or desire.

(The Free Dictionary)

Mariah's Story

Mariah is lying across her bed on a Saturday night reminiscing about some of the good times she shared with Nick. Flashbacks flood her memory of the sexy candlelit bubble baths and slow dancing together in the kitchen while making dinner. Mariah picks up her cell phone and scrolls through her photo album to look at pictures of her and Nick together on their romantic trip to Jamaica. Before she knows it Mariah impulsively sends Nick a text saying, "Hey!"—to which she receives no response. With her feelings crushed and a pang of regret, she calls her sister, Whitney, for advice. Whitney picks up on the second ring.

WHITNEY: "Hey, Sis! How was your day?"

MARIAH: "I think I did something really, really stupid, Whitney!"

WHITNEY: "What?"

MARIAH: "I just texted Nick and he never responded. I feel like such an idiot!"

WHITNEY: "What did you text him?"

MARIAH: Hesitantly she responds. "Hey!"

WHITNEY: "That's it? What were you doing? A temperature check?"

MARIAH: "I guess. I…I was looking at pictures of us on vacation in Jamaica and got caught up in the moment."

WHITNEY: "Yeah, Jamaica memories will do it every time." She laughs. "Don't beat yourself up. You miss him. I get it. We all have a weak moment every now and then. But you have to distance yourself because you cannot move on with your life if Nick is still in it."

MARIAH: "I know…I know."

WHITNEY: "That means NO calling, NO texting, and especially NO checking Nick's social media pages. I know my baby sister. All you will be doing is setting yourself up to get your feelings hurt by stalking his Facebook page, looking for a relationship status change and trying to analyze every picture that he posts."

MARIAH: "You're right. I am definitely driving myself crazy. Nick posted a vacation picture last week and even though there was no woman in sight, I obsessed over what woman he *may* have traveled with. Then, I tried to compare his Facebook pictures with the pictures of us together to see if he looked happier in our pictures. It was maddening *and* exhausting! I have to get off the crazy train." Mariah laughs at her own realization.

WHITNEY: "Could you, right now, delete Nick's phone number and all the text history on your phone and on Facebook?"

MARIAH: "Oh my goodness! I don't think so."

WHITNEY: "If that makes you anxious or it feels too extreme, try deleting him from your phone after you write down his contact information. Then fold the paper several times and save it in a Ziplock baggie filled with water and put it in the freezer. If you later have a moment of weakness and want to call or text him, you will have ample time to think whether it is worth it or not."

MARIAH: "I can do that."

WHITNEY: "Good! This is part of the healing process. I want you to think about something. When someone breaks up with a person they love, most likely they have been thinking about it for weeks, months or even years. They did not just wake up that morning and decide they wanted out of the relationship. So by the time they tell the person they are breaking up with—they have emotionally checked out. Nick is five steps ahead of you in his healing."

MARIAH: "I just need to work on me."

WHITNEY: "Yes, you do."

It's Important To Know

Desperate for Closure. You will most likely experience a desperate need for answers from your ex. If you cannot get the answers from him, you might seek out your ex's family, friends, or coworkers—which may or may not be a wise decision. We often yearn for closure because we inherently understand the world through a past, present and future narrative. Most healthy relationships have a good sense of where they have been, where they are and where they are going. However, when a one-sided breakup occurs unexpectedly in a seemingly secure and serious relationship, it traumatically thrusts that person being broken up with from a safe psychological place into an abyss. By knowing the reasons why the relationship was not working, the initiator of the breakup has the advantage because he has already sorted out his story—things make sense for him.

What is Closure? Closure is the piece needed for us to restructure our narrative in a healthy way through understanding what went wrong and reconfiguring the story accordingly. When we are refused closure, then we are often left to wonder: What did I do? How could someone I thought I knew so well do this to me? How can I trust myself to make good decisions in the future?

Try not to personalize the rejection. Oftentimes, the flaw is in the other person but we automatically assume something is wrong with us. Your ex may have had an inability to commit, was immature, too busy, or it was just not the right time for him.

When You Don't Get Closure. If you do not get closure from your ex or the answers given to you from him are meant to tear you down as a person, then one technique to adopt is to create your own closure scenario. How do you do that, you ask? It is simple. Let's revisit Nick and Mariah's situation. Mariah senses that there is something deeper to the reason that Nick gives for why he changed his mind about marriage. Maybe Nick does not want any further conflict or maybe he does not want to send Mariah off the deep end and just gives her a simple "It's not you... It's me" explanation and nothing more. In this situation, Mariah needs to create her own closure story which may be that Nick is afraid of true commitment. Whether it is true or not—it does not matter. It is the narrative that Mariah can have peace with, and she can move to the next phase of letting go and accepting that the relationship is over.

Your personal closure story can be anything you feel. Here are a few suggestions:

- ❤️ He was mentally unstable and unable to give me what I needed out of the relationship.
- ❤️ He was pathological liar and I deserved better.
- ❤️ He was a narcissist and I was tired of being manipulated.
- ❤️ He fell out of love and I did not want to be with someone who did not love me.

💔 The distance was too much.

💔 He was physically abusive, and I deserved better.

💔 He had a fear of commitment.

💔 We were not equally yoked.

💔 We were not sexually compatible.

💔 He could not afford me. Some men want a Bentley, but they can't afford the maintenance of a Bentley.

💔 He chose a different lifestyle that I did not want to be a part of.

Make a Clean Break. After the breakup, it is important to tie up loose ends as soon as possible to start the healing. Avoid keeping anything or leaving anything that can be asked for later on. If you still have some of his personal things—clothing, CDs, appliances, books, furniture—return them. If there are things you left behind, ask for them once more. If you have no luck in getting the items back, forget it and move on.

Your Ex Does Not Care. You may feel the need to express to your ex how you feel through text, email or a call. But the truth is that your ex does not care how you feel. His reality is one of relief that the relationship is over. The circumstances had not been working for him and he can now move on. Anything you say is not going to change his mind, so save your dignity. If you both travel in the same social circle and have mutual friends—you especially do not want to look desperate and have people whispering about you at the next social gathering.

Apply the 'No Contact' Rule. The concept is simple. Have **nothing** to do with your ex. It is not recommended to still have an intimate relationship after you have broken up. Start weaning yourself off him as soon as possible—both emotionally and physically. This may be easier said than done, but cut all social media connections (Facebook, Snap Chat, Instagram, WhatsApp...etc.) and all booty calls. If you have children together or work together, you may still need to text or speak with each other, but try to limit contact to the necessary basics. You may have to avoid or screen calls from unknown numbers or mutual friends for a while. Once you block him, he may find other ways to contact you.

No Sex with the Ex. This is part of the 'No Contact' rule— but needs its own sub-category for clarity and emphasis. You may have the urge to lure your ex back with sex. There is no such thing as "friends with benefits." Continuing the physical relationship after giving up the committed relationship is a prescription for trouble. The sex will not mend your broken heart, and you will be setting yourself up for major guilt and disappointment when you ultimately don't get what you want. The rule should be—if the relationship is dead, bury it. Don't sleep with it.

Physical Withdrawal. If you were used to spatial closeness and lots of physical touch with your ex— hugging, cuddling, sexual intimacy—then you may experience physical withdrawal from that after the breakup. This is real. Some suggestions that can lessen the withdrawal effects are:

- 💔 get a weekly body massage so your body gets the touch it was accustomed to
- 💔 hug your friends
- 💔 hug your dog or cat (if it lets you)
- 💔 exercise or take a walk.

Chemical Withdrawal. Licensed psychologist Dr. Wyatt Fisher explains that the brain releases surges of dopamine and oxytocin when in love, which light up the brain's reward center (like cocaine). This chemical neuro-illumination is due to all that emotional and physical intimacy experienced in relationships, which all feels super great. But what happens when we fall out of love? "When a person goes through a breakup, the brain experiences massive withdrawal symptoms almost identical to a heroin addict quitting cold turkey," says Dr. Fisher. "After a breakup, people should expect withdrawal symptoms for roughly six months and increase their self-care and social support during this season." Of course, you should always seek professional help if things feel too out of hand.

Desire to Get Your Ex Back. Your heart hurts and you still love him. I get it. Because of this love you may want to try to work things out with your ex. There are many websites, videos, and books around that sell you the narrative that if you do "this one thing" you can get your ex back. I want you to stop and ask yourself this one question: "Why do I want to be with someone that does not want to be with me?" The lion never comes back to lick the bones after devouring the meat.

Let's Do The Work

Journal Questions

1. Do you still call or text your ex? Does he respond? Does your ex randomly call you? How does it make you feel?

_____

_____

_____

_____

2. Are you still intimate with your ex? If so, describe your feelings after each encounter.

_____

_____

_____

_____

3. Are you still connected to your ex on social media? How are you handling it?

_____

_____

_____

_____

The Closure Exercise

Are you struggling with not getting closure from your ex? That is normal. Let's work through this together. In your journal, answer the following questions:

1. Did you get a reason for the breakup from your ex? If so, what was it? If not, how does that make you feel?

2. If your ex did not provide closure or it was a lame excuse, what is your own closure story that you have created?

3. You may still have that nagging urge to hear a satisfying reason from your ex. How would you feel if you reach out to your ex, and he does not respond to your attempts for a closure conversation? Would this put you in a better or worse place emotionally?

4. What percent of you is secretly hoping your ex will want to get back together?

5. What questions do you still have for your ex?

6. What specifically do you want closure around? (This could be your ex's reason for the split, something they said during the breakup conversation, or reasons/explanations for past actions or hurts.)

7. What could your ex say to bring you closure or greater understanding of the breakup?

8. Why would these words bring you closure? How would those words impact you, or be meaningful?

Affirmation to Recite

"I allow myself to let go of things to get stronger every day."

Movie Time Recommendation

Fatal Attraction
(1987) *1h 59min* Rated R
Drama/Thriller

Spoiler Alert

The synopsis below may give away important plot points.

Dan Gallagher (Michael Douglas) is a successful, happily married New York attorney living in Manhattan when he meets Alexandra (Alex) Forrest (Glenn Close), an editor for a publishing company. While his wife, Beth (Anne Archer), and daughter, Ellen (Ellen Hamilton Latzen), are out of town for the weekend, Dan has a passionate affair with Alex. Though he thought it was understood to be a simple fling, she begins clinging to him.

Dan explains that he must go home and Alex cuts her wrists in a suicide attempt. Dan helps her to bandage her wrists and later leaves. He thinks the affair is forgotten, but she shows up at various places to see him. She waits at his office one day to apologize and invites him to the opera Madam Butterfly, but he turns her down. She then calls his office until he tells his secretary to no longer take her calls. Alex then calls his home at all hours and informs him that she is pregnant and plans to keep the baby. Although he wants nothing to do with her, she argues that he must take responsibility. She shows up at his apartment (which is for sale) and meets Beth, as she pretends to be a buyer. Later that night, Dan goes to Alex's apartment to confront her about her actions. In response, she replies that she will not be ignored.

Dan moves his family to the New York village of Bedford, but this does not deter Alex. She stalks him in a parking garage, pours acid on his vehicle and follows him home one night to spy on him, Beth and Ellen from the bushes in his yard. The sight of his family life makes Alex sick to her stomach. Her obsession escalates. Dan approaches the police to apply for a restraining order against her.

At one point, while the Gallaghers are not home, Alex kills Ellen's pet rabbit and puts it on their stove to boil. After this, Dan tells Beth about the affair and Alex's pregnancy. Beth gets enraged and asks Dan to leave. Before he goes, Dan calls Alex to tell her that Beth knows about the affair. Beth gets on the phone and warns Alex that if she persists, she will kill her. Without Dan and Beth's knowledge, Alex picks up Ellen from school and takes her to an amusement park, buying her ice cream and taking her on a roller coaster. Beth panics when she realizes that she does not know where Ellen is. Beth drives around searching for Ellen and rear-ends a car stopped at an intersection. She is injured and hospitalized.

Dan barges into Alex's apartment and attacks her, choking her but stops short of strangling her. Alex lunges at him with a kitchen knife but he overpowers her, puts the knife down and leaves with Alex sitting on the floor, smiling. Dan approaches the police about having her arrested, but the police say they lack cause to take action against her.

Following Beth's release from the hospital, she forgives Dan and they return home.

Beth prepares a bath for herself and Alex suddenly appears with a kitchen knife. Alex starts to explain her resentment of Beth, nervously fidgeting and slightly cutting her own leg with the knife and then attacks Beth. Alex and Beth struggle. Dan hears the screaming and runs in, wrestles Alex into the bathtub and seemingly drowns her. She suddenly emerges from the water, swinging the knife. Beth, who went searching for Dan's gun, shoots Alex in the chest, killing her. The final scene shows police cars outside the Gallaghers' house. As Dan finishes talking with the cops, he walks inside, where Beth is waiting for him. They embrace and proceed upstairs as the camera focuses on a picture of Dan, Beth, and Ellen.

Chapter 5

DEPRESSION

- Experiencing symptoms like sleep and appetite disturbance, intense sadness, loneliness and crying spells
- This phase can feel like it will last forever

Depression is defined as feelings of severe sadness, unhappiness, and dejection.

(The Oxford Dictionary)

Mariah's Story

Before the breakup, Mariah was a happy and very social person who loved life. She had a full calendar of brunches with the girls and networking events for business. But now she is having a hard time just getting out of bed, and activities that used to bring her joy seem pointless. Mariah decides to make an appointment to see her therapist, Dr. Portia Anderson.

MARIAH: "Hello, I'm here for my 1 o'clock with Dr. Anderson." Mariah is at her scheduled therapy appointment to get help with sorting out her mind and emotions. It has become too much for her to handle on her own.

TINA: "Yes, Ms. Carson. Please sign in. Has any of your information changed? Address, insurance, emergency contact?"

MARIAH: "Oh, yeah. I guess I have to change my emergency contact info." She winces at that being another reminder.

TINA: "No problem. Here is a new form to fill out. Dr. A. will be with you shortly. Would you like a bottle of water while you wait?"

MARIAH: "No, thank you. I'm fine." After filling out the form, Mariah takes a seat in the waiting room. She picks up the latest edition of PEOPLE Magazine and begins thumbing through it.

DR. A: A few moments later, "Hi Mariah! Please come back!"

MARIAH: "Hi Dr. A. "Mariah follows Dr. Anderson back to her office and sits down on the sofa.

DR. A: "So it has been over a year since we last had a session. What brings you in to see me today?"

MARIAH: "Well, I recently went through a traumatic breakup with my fiancé Nick and I feel very much off kilter. It's like I am walking in a fog and I can't get my balance. Plus, I am sad. Really, really, *really* sad."

DR. A: "How recent are we talking?"

MARIAH: "About four months ago. It's still fresh. Everything reminds me of him, and it is so painful." Mariah pauses and then continues. "I can't listen to the radio or my once-favorite playlist on my phone. As I drive around the neighborhood, I remember us walking for exercise or working out at the gym together."

DR. A: "How are you functioning daily? On a scale from 1 to 10, with 10 being highly functional."

MARIAH: "I am probably a 3 or 4. I'm finding it difficult to concentrate at work, which is affecting my performance. I'm not sleeping well. All I feel like doing is staying in bed with the covers over my head and the blinds shut. I replay details of the relationship over and over trying to figure out what went wrong and at what exact point did things start to shift. I've been avoiding the grocery stores because we used to have a weekly shopping ritual and it makes me sad to walk down the aisles by myself. I guess the positive side is that I have lost those 15 pounds that I had been struggling with for the past three years!"

DR. A: "What you are experiencing is grief from the heartbreak and it is a normal reaction. I just read about how the Asian people do their grieving and what they do is they create a ritual where they spend an hour every evening just thinking about what they won't have anymore in the future. Likewise, you would *only* think about and grieve the future without Nick— no wedding, no children, no sharing a bed or home anymore, no 'plus one' at social events... etc. Once you start saying bad things to yourself—like 'I am not lovable'— you have to stop the ritual, or it will become detrimental to you."

MARIAH: "That sounds like something my sister was telling me about, but more intense."

DR. A: "It *can* be intense. In that hour you are crying and grieving the loss of the future that you would have had with him and then you grieve all the things that you both talked about doing in the future. You think about just that—letting the sadness come to the surface. I hope that was helpful."

MARIAH: "Yes, very much so. I can set aside an hour at night to do this."

DR. A: "In my own battle with depression and with other people, I would notice that there is this vortex that kind of starts at the top that spirals down to this really awful place. And it usually starts with some thought…that thought about yourself at the top of that vortex like 'I'm not lovable,' 'It must be me,' 'What's wrong with me?' If that starts—it is almost like this slippery slope, right down to this whirlpool. "

MARIAH: "Yes, I can sooooo relate."

DR. A: "So one of the things that I still have to do sometimes is pay attention to where the vortex starts. Which thought is triggering that downward spiral into the bad depression? Learn to pay attention to that thought and reverse it right away. And you just avoid the spiral."

MARIAH: "Yes. Yes. How do I reverse that negative thought?"

DR. A: "There's a skill I will call Baby Steps that is based on Dialectical Behavior Therapy by psychologist Marsha Linehan. It starts with us recognizing that there is an area of our brain that keeps us going forward toward rewards or treats. So you create some little vision of something that makes you smile and laugh—like the hand of God coming out of the sky giving you a high-five or cheerleaders spelling out your name, letter by letter—or the stadium people chanting your name to get you going."

MARIAH: "I like that!"

DR. A: "Now one woman said that her little boy would say this really funny phrase and she would always imagine her little boy saying this funny phrase. It starts to become a mental reward. Then you set these teeny tiny goals to get yourself out of bed and moving because motivation comes after action, not before."

MARIAH: "Oh…I need to jot that down! '*Motivation comes after action, not before.*'"

DR. A: "Most of us operate in this mindset of 'I'm not motivated.' But the truth is that you must put yourself in action mode for motivation. So what you would need to do, let's say you are on the sofa and can't get yourself moving.

You then set the tiny goal to stand up and you stand up and then the stadium people chant in your head and it makes you smile. And then the next goal might be to walk across the room and then God gives you a high-five. The next might be changing your clothes. But if the step is too big, don't take it."

MARIAH: "I can relate."

DR. A: "Good. Because if the step is too big, you need to break it down into smaller steps with little mental rewards that make you laugh or smile. And that way, once the action starts to happen, the motivation kicks in! At some point, even if you have to take baby steps to get yourself clear out of the car, to head to the gym—whatever it is—somewhere along the way motivation will kick in because you are taking action."

MARIAH: "Thank you, Dr. A.! This is really helpful information for anyone in a depressed state to get themselves moving."

It's Important To Know

Give Yourself Permission to Feel Your Feelings. Do not let anyone tell you how you should feel or that you should "get over it" and "move on." It is a process. If you choose to suppress your feelings, it could easily lead to bigger problems down the road like clinical depression, anxiety, substance abuse, and other health issues.

You May Experience Intense Sadness. This depressive phase feels like it will last forever. But it is an appropriate response to the loss of a serious relationship. You will withdraw from life, feeling like you are in a fog of intense sadness. You will cry daily. You will want to stay in bed with the covers over your head and blinds shut. However, if it has been longer than three months in this phase, start looking for a therapist or counselor to see. You need professional help to guide you through the wilderness and there is nothing wrong with that!

You may Experience Loss of Meaning

- 💔 Goals and dreams (for the future have been shattered)
- 💔 Faith (may be questioned)
- 💔 Will/desire to live (...you may ask, "Why go on...?")
- 💔 Joy (may be hard to find)

HOLD ON!!

Stay Busy. Keeping your mind off your situation is beneficial. Often when you are doing for others, you are not thinking about your own problems. If you have young children, force yourself to spend time with them— engage in their sporting events or hobbies. Also, volunteering at a non-profit organization gets you out of the house into another environment and you can be a blessing to other people which should uplift your spirit.

Your Weight will Fluctuate. Most likely you will lose your appetite and weight will just fall off or you will gain weight during this heartbreak cycle.

Your Sleep Pattern will Change. You may find yourself sleeping more or finding it hard to sleep. This unhealthy sleep pattern is a sign of depression and can wreak havoc on your mind.

Be Aware of Dangerous Residual Patterns:

- 💔 Excessive shopping—can lead to unnecessary debt
- 💔 Drinking to numb the pain and escape
- 💔 Doing drugs to numb the pain and escape
- 💔 Risky sexual behavior to numb the pain and temporarily satisfy that feeling of being wanted/ needed/desired
- 💔 Gambling—can lead to financial hardship

Be Aware of Any "Acceptable Death" Thoughts or Sucidal Thoughts. The pain and grief may be so intense that you start to wish you would get into a car accident or wish you would get a terminal disease so you could just die. These thoughts of "acceptable" ways to die are just the precursor to more serious suicidal thoughts. However, if you are feeling hopeless and having suicidal thoughts of taking your own life, you are not alone.

💔 Know that you can and will get through this.

💔 Ask for help immediately. If you find yourself in this space, please call a licensed therapist or contact the **National Suicide Prevention Lifeline at: 1-800-273-8255 or text _GO_ to 741741** to reach a trained Crisis Counselor through Crisis Text Line, a global not-for-profit organization.

💔 Think of all the people who love you and care about you. Make a list.

💔 Think of all the things you have yet to do, whether it is to get married, travel to a foreign country, write that book that will change people's lives, see your child graduate, etc.

HOLD ON!!

Re-establish Good Self-Care. Self-care is defined as giving attention to your physical and psychological well-being. You may be feeling like you do not want to get out of bed, let alone shower, brush your teeth, brush your hair, and get dressed. But you need to try. The following are other examples of positive self-care activities:

- 💔 Listen to your favorite (uplifting) music
- 💔 Take a warm bath
- 💔 Get a restful night's sleep
- 💔 Exercise
- 💔 Eat something healthy
- 💔 Spend time with people that build you up and make you happy
- 💔 Do something that makes you smile

Stop Saying Bad Things to Yourself. Words are powerful. Avoid saying negative thing to yourself. Notice if you are thinking things like "I can never …" or "Why am I so unlovable?" or "I am just no good at…" Or "I made a mess of…" If you are, then stop thinking or saying it the moment you are aware of it. Then go a step further and take a moment to think about what you appreciate about yourself. Think about your character. Some examples of things you appreciate about yourself may be:

- 💔 Generous
- 💔 Loyal
- 💔 Good cook
- 💔 Kind

- 💔 Intelligent
- 💔 Good peacekeeper
- 💔 Good work ethic
- 💔 Patient
- 💔 Considerate of others
- 💔 Organized
- 💔 Follow through on commitments
- 💔 Prompt
- 💔 Good eye for decorating
- 💔 Great mother
- 💔 Great listener

After you have made your list, carry it with you and read it as needed.

Make Time to Exercise. Exercise is probably the single most effective "depression-defeater" you can do. It is the best way to overcome lethargy.

Research has shown that exercise raises levels of serotonin in the brain. Serotonin is the main body chemical associated with feelings of happiness, relaxation, and self-confidence. Additionally, Serotonin increases blood flow to the brain, which is associated with many aspects of healthy brain activity. For people who are not already regular exercisers, the biggest problem may be getting started. Here are some helpful tips:

- 💔 Educate yourself on the importance of exercise.
- 💔 Find a type of exercise you enjoy.
- 💔 Identify what times you have available to exercise.
- 💔 Join a gym.
- 💔 Get a personal trainer, if possible. If not, get a workout buddy.
- 💔 Commit to an action plan.
- 💔 Be accountable. Keep track of what you do. Look into getting a phone App to help you.

Benefits of Physical Exercise as a treatment for depression:

- 💔 Helps to keep the stress hormones normal and relieves stress.
- 💔 Has a positive effect on your mood.
- 💔 Helps to manage your weight.
- 💔 Promotes growth of new brain cells and regulates brain chemicals (neurotransmitters).
- 💔 Builds endurance and physical strength, which combats fatigue.

💔 Helps to overcome the sedentary lifestyle that often comes with depression.

💔 Releases the "feel good" hormones (endorphins).

💔 Increases your social contacts (in an exercise class or in neighborhood or health club interactions).

💔 Improves the overall sense of well-being.

💔 Improves the quality of your sleep, which in turn improves your mood.

Isolation versus Solitude. Resist self-imposed isolation. All alone time is not the same. Solitude, rather than isolation, has a purpose and provides a sense of fulfillment and enjoyment. It allows you to relax, self-reflect and think or replenish yourself when feeling overwhelmed. Solitude is something you choose to experience, in contrast to the isolation of depression. We all need a bit of alone time in our lives. Reading a good book or your favorite magazine, taking a jog on a nature trail, or journaling are all examples of solitude that is important to your overall well-being. Even though solitude is alone time, it is not the same as the isolation and withdrawal that comes with depression. If you find yourself avoiding people and activities for no reason, that is withdrawal. Avoiding isolation when depressed is a challenge. Push yourself—make that conscious effort— to get out and be with others. Get out of bed and go to the grocery store. Have small talk with the cashier or the store clerk. Make it a point to return phone calls from friends and family who are positive and supportive. Eventually it will all become easier to do.

Let's Do The Work

The Self-Test Exercise

If you are wondering if you are experiencing depression, the following self-test can help you learn more about yourself. Your responses will not give you a diagnosis but can provide insight to what you are feeling. Remember, there is no substitute for the opinions and advice of a professional mental health therapist or physician. Check all the statements that are true for you:

Feelings

- I feel sad and irritable much of the time.
- I feel hopeless most of the time.
- I cry all of the time.
- I hate myself.
- I feel lonely most of the time.
- I cannot seem to get along with anyone.
- I have trouble making decisions.
- I have trouble concentrating and remembering things.
- Other people have noticed changes in my moods.
- Nothing is interesting to me.

Behaviors

- I sometimes use alcohol and drugs to cope.
- My performance at work is declining.
- I have lost interest in activities I once enjoyed.
- I avoid places I used to go that now make me feel uncomfortable.
- I do not want to get out of the bed.

Health and Well-being

- I sometimes think about suicide and ending it all.
- I have planned to commit suicide.
- I have attempted suicide.
- I have trouble with sleep—I either sleep too much or not enough.
- I have trouble with my appetite—I either eat too much or not enough.

Checking any one of these items as true for you does not mean you are suffering from depression. However, if you have checked more than one, it is a good idea to talk with someone about how you are feeling. If you have checked several, please talk to someone right away—a doctor, a mental therapist, a trusted friend or a family member.

If you have been thinking about suicide, I encourage you to call a doctor, emergency room, or 911 right away to get immediate help. You can also call and speak to a professional at the **National Suicide Prevention Lifeline at 1-800-784-2433**.

Get Interested In Life Again

💔 Try to learn one new thing each day: a new word, a new fact, a new recipe, or something that you did not know about a friend or colleague. Expanding your knowledge ignites a new spark of excitement and it can help build your self-esteem. You may be surprised by the satisfaction you get from learning new things.

💔 Explore new tastes. Try a new food, read a different genre of book, or listen to a type of music you would not normally listen to. Psychologists say that you need to repeat the new "taste" experience five times before you get to like it—so do not give up too soon. You may surprise yourself!

💔 Take up a new hobby, sport, or pastime. When you find one you like, search for a discussion group on the internet or join a local group that shares your interest.

Journal Exercise

Intentionally Increase Your Positive Experiences. Depression robs us of our joy and makes it difficult for us to see the simple pleasures in life. When you are depressed, you tend to avoid contact with positive experiences because your body is low on norepinephrine for energy and dopamine for good feelings. It is easy to disengage from what we would have otherwise enjoyed and then before you know it, we are on a downward spiral into an abyss, with no brakes.

How do we counteract this, you ask? The first part is to **be aware** of the positive things in your life and then maximize contact with those positive experiences or people. Try the following exercise:

1. Keep track of every activity you do for a few days.
2. Answer this question for each activity: "Was it pleasurable or unpleasurable?" You must pick one. Even if you

are inclined to say, "Well, it wasn't *unpleasurable*," the way many that are depressed would answer—the correct answer would be "pleasurable."

3. For each pleasurable activity, rate the degree of pleasure from 1-10, with 1 being the least amount of pleasure and 10 being the most.

Take note of the things you get pleasure from in your life no matter how depressed you are. You may take pleasure in a hot shower, or in your pet greeting you when you get home, getting a big hug or watching your child practice soccer.

Next, **enhance** those pleasurable experiences. This is not so difficult. If taking a hot bath is pleasurable, can it be even more pleasurable if you play music in the bathroom, or light a candle, or add some bubbles or bath salts? This same technique can apply to meeting a friend for coffee (make sure to order a specialty coffee you enjoy), taking a short walk (notice the colors of the sky or the neighbor's flowers or hug a tree along the way), talking to the kids after school (review in your mind your child's smile after the chat is over), and so on. By enhancing the pleasurable things you are already doing, you will boost the dopamine and consequently feel happier. The downward spiral starts to reverse.

We each have our own idea of a pleasurable experience or activity. Here are a few examples:

Spend time with friends	Volunteer	Travel	Do a jigsaw puzzle
Play with a pet	Relax	Watch sports	Knit, quilt, crochet
Cook	Stretch	Get a massage	Read a good book
Reach a goal	Sing	Window shop	Get your hair done
Watch a funny movie	Garden	Go to a party	Go to a museum
Listen to Music	Laugh	Give a gift	Spend time with family
Eat a good meal	Meditate	Do Sudoku	Plan a party

Affirmation to Recite

"I have light to shine onto the world, and I allow it to flow out of me."

Movie Time Recommendation

It's Kind of a Funny Story

(2010) *1hr 41min* Rated PG-13

Comedy/Drama/Romance

Spoiler Alert

The synopsis below may give away important plot points.

You would not think a movie set in a mental health hospital could be heartwarming, but this one is. This well-crafted film tells the story of 16-year-old Craig (Keir Gilchrist) who checks himself into a psychiatric ward because of his depression and ideas of suicide. He ends up staying in the adult unit because the youth wing is under renovation. The hospital is not a scary place and the patients are not portrayed as "mad" or "insane"—it is a safe place where people who are struggling are getting help, and using humor as a relief from some of the serious conditions that brought them there. This Hollywood approach to a psychiatric unit may be more comical than any real-life scenario, but it helps to normalize the fact that sometimes people need this level of care.

THE BREAKUP PIVOT

Chapter 6

ACCEPTANCE

- Comes with accepting the reality that the relationship is over
- You choose to move on with your life

Acceptance in human psychology is defined as a person's assent to the reality of the situation without attempting to change it or protest it, allowing unwanted private experiences (thoughts, feelings and urges) to come and go without struggling with them.

(Wikipedia.org)

Mariah's Story

It is a sunny day in April and Mariah gets a call from her old college roommate, Jena. Jena is engaged and is in the initial planning stages for her upcoming wedding in May of the following year.

JENA: "Happy Easter, Mariah!!"

MARIAH: "Happy Easter to you too, Jena! It's so great to hear from you."

JENA: "It's been a while. How are you doing? What's been going on?"

MARIAH: "Well, the biggest change is that I'm no longer with Nick. It's been a little over a year now."

JENA: "What?!! You two broke up?"

MARIAH: "Yup. He didn't want to get married."

JENA: "Dang! I'm so sorry to hear that. Are you good?"

MARIAH: "I no longer have that intense anger or sadness, thank goodness. But I do have moments of hurt and loneliness every now and then. When that feeling comes, I just

	try to remind myself that Nick was just one of many lessons in my life and God has greater things for me."
JENA:	"That's right! You had to tow the old broken-down car out of the driveway to make room for the new car." Jena and Mariah laugh at her analogy.
MARIAH:	"Enough about me…What's new with you?"
JENA:	"Well, Scott and I are planning a destination wedding and I would be honored to have you be a bridesmaid. The wedding is going to be in Aruba next May!" Jena and Mariah both squeal with excitement.
MARIAH:	"Ooooh, Aruba! Sounds like so much fun. Count me in! At least one of us will be married." Mariah laughs.
JENA:	"We are going to have a blast, girl! I'm so excited that you are part of my bride squad. I will send you the resort details to your email."
MARIAH:	"I'll start saving up!"

It's Important To Know

According to *Be Mindful & Stress Free* by Gina M. Biegel, pain just sometimes wants to be heard. She highlights certain blocking behaviors that we tend to use that do not allow us to heal.

You must get past these blocking behaviors to get to the acceptance phase:

- **Pushing away the pain**. Example: Filling almost every waking moment with something to do. Staying so busy that you hardly have time to think about the breakup.
- **Denying what happened**. Example: Not telling people that you and your ex broke up—not wanting to accept it.
- **Holding on or clinging to the pain**. Example: Looking at old happy and romantic photos of the two of you together on vacation but they just make you feel worse.

💔 **Ruminating or obsessing about the pain**. Example: You cannot stop thinking about how you are not good enough or what you did wrong in the relationship. Or you constantly go over text messages or voicemails from your ex.

💔 **Engaging in negative self-talk**. Example: Beating yourself up for not being thinner, richer, prettier, or smarter. "If only I were__, my ex would have stayed."

💔 **Feeling guilt or shame about what happened**. Example: Thinking the breakup is all your fault and you feel bad about it.

Acceptance is Not Always Easy. However, when you learn to accept things as they are, especially if they are out of your control, you will begin to feel lighter and start to heal.

Acceptance is Learning to Live with Your New Norm. You are forging a new chapter in your life without your ex being a factor. Be patient with yourself and do not expect to reach the acceptance phase quickly. The process could take years. You could also ebb in and out of the acceptance phase.

Your Ex Broke Up with You For a Reason. Accept that you may never know the whole truth. The harsh reality is that people do not leave people they love unless there is a compelling reason. Whether you want to accept it or not, the pain of staying in the relationship outweighed the pain of leaving for your ex.

You Are at Peace. You will have accepted that the relationship has ended when you stop thinking that you will get back with your ex. When only good memories remain and you no longer feel bitter or any blame, you have reached the acceptance phase.

Valuable Lessons were Learned. Appreciate the lessons you learned in the relationship and make peace with the fact that your ex is no longer in your life.

Helpful Strategies to Move on From the Past. Quick fact—you will constantly deal with memories, places, and thoughts that remind you of the life you once lived when you were with your ex. Here are a few tips to help you move into the future:

- 💔 Stay away from old hangouts for a while.
- 💔 For a period, do not listen to songs that are reminders of your past.

❣ Begin to create new memories with your friends or your kids. Take photos and put them around the house.

❣ Create a vision board to depict your new wishes, dreams and goals. Take a picture of the completed vision board with your phone so you can have it available to look at when not at home.

Get Excited About the Future. A year from now, where do you want to be? More importantly, *who* do you want to be? Design a new vision for your life, which could include travel, learning new languages, even going back to school or trying a totally different vocation. It is all up to you.

Let's Do The Work

Journal Questions

1. How do you describe your breakup pain to others? What key words really tell the story?

_____

_____

_____

_____

2. What lessons did you learn from your relationship?

_____

_____

_____

_____

3. If you could give a name to your breakup pain, what would it be? You could name it after a movie character, a color, an object, or even a feeling—choose any name you want, and feel free to get creative.

_____

_____

_____

_____

4. How does the chosen name make you feel? Hopeful? Victimized? Empowered? Sad? Demoralized? Intimidated? Powerful? In control? Out of control?

_____

_____

_____

_____

5. If the previous name you came up with for your breakup pain produced negative feelings, come up with a new name. Think of a word or name that might make you smile, laugh, or feel less negative. Again, draw upon TV, film, and other ideas, as well as objects.

_____

_____

_____

_____

6. What would life be like if you did not have to carry your breakup pain?

_____

_____

_____

_____

7. What part or parts of the breakup "story" can you begin to accept?

_____

_____

_____

_____

8. How might an attitude of acceptance change how you feel? How would it change the story you tell others about your pain? Write that new story below—even if you are not entirely committed to it or believe it. Just see what it would look like and sound like.

_____

_____

_____

_____

Affirmation to Recite

"I am a better person from the hardships I have gone through."

Movie Time Recommendation

Legally Blonde

(2001) *1h 36min* Rated PG-13

Comedy /Romance

Spoiler Alert

The synopsis below may give away important plot points.

Elle Woods (Reese Witherspoon) has it all. She is the president of her sorority, a Hawaiian Tropic girl, Miss June in her campus calendar, and, above all, a natural blonde. She dates the cutest fraternity boy on campus and wants nothing more than to be Mrs. Warner Huntington III. But there is just one thing stopping Warner (Matthew Davis) from popping the question: Elle is too blonde. Growing up across the street from Aaron Spelling might mean something in Los Angeles, California, but means nothing to Warner's East Coast blue blood family. So, Warner dumps Elle before heading off to Harvard law school to reunite with an old sweetheart from prep school. Elle rallies all of her resources and gets into Harvard, determined to win Warner back. Law school proves to be a far cry from the comforts of her poolside and the mall. Elle must wage the battle of her life for her guy, for herself and for all the blondes who suffer endless indignities every day.

Conclusion

Congratulations on getting this far on your journey to healing and wholeness! You now have an intimate understanding of the phases of heartbreak grief: shock, denial, anger, desperate for answers and/or contact, depression and acceptance and how to manage through them.

How do you feel?

_____

_____

_____

_____

If you could choose a chapter that you related to the most, which would it be and why?

_____

_____

_____

_____

If you could choose a chapter that has helped you the most, which would it be and how did it help?

_____

_____

_____

_____

_____

Coming Next:

The Breakup Pivot
Volume II: The Healing Process

I am so grateful that you took this journey with me and now it is time to go to the next level! There is something waiting beyond what you are experiencing right now. The next level is Healing. Will it be easy? No. Worth it? Absolutely! Let's get there together. You are incredibly brave, strong, courageous and deserve the life of your own design.

- 💔 Forgiveness
- 💔 Unpacking the Baggage

THE BREAKUP PIVOT

- 💔 Overcoming Anxiety and Fear
- 💔 Ending the Sabotage Cycle
- 💔 And more...

Acknowledgements

First and foremost, I would like to thank God for making a way for this book to be written. I also would like to thank my cousin Claytee White and my friend Charmaine Carter for the continued encouragement to pen this book and to be a light in the darkness for many women going through a breakup. I would like to thank Celine Rollins, one of my best friends of 32 years who passed away in 2020, for her love and support over the years, and my other friends and family— Candyce Partee-Stewart, Sharon Baker, Renee White, Mishele Walker, Tammy Young, Gilda Alston, Jena Baker-Calloway, Karen Bell, Cyril Hanson III, Talya Shirley, Victoria Trussell, Dr. Betty Ruth Baptist Jones, MD, Ph.D., Gloria Baptist, Marian Parker, Sharon Partee, Michele Partee, Lenore Partee Boyd, Keva Partee, Jocelyn Gunn, Amber Parker, Kimberly Terrell, JoAnn Blassingame, Christina Blassingame, Chamise Carter, Tracey Webster, Amber Smiley, Raquel James, Tenecia Harris, Angela Jenkins, Shana Laster, Montoya Craighead, Dr. Cindy Milligan, Brianna Barbour, and my Aunt Dora Jackson and Aunt Margaret Jones—for their support and their unique part in getting this book completed.

Resources

The wisdom and thought-provoking information in several books, on websites, and from various organizations guided me in writing this book. Many of the resources used and cited in *The Breakup Pivot: Overcoming Heartbreak*, as well as related recommended resources, are referenced below by chapter.

Introduction

- Wolfelt, Alan D. Ph.D. *The Wilderness of Grief-Finding Your Way*. Fort Collins, CO: Companion Press, 2007.
- Kubler-Ross M.D., Elisabeth. *On Death & Dying-What the Dying Have to Teach Doctors, Nurses, Clergy & Their Own Families. (50ᵀʰ Anniversary Edition)*. New York, NY: Scribner Publisher, 2014.
- Elliott, Susan J. *Getting Past Your Breakup*. Cambridge, MA: Da Capo Press, 2009.
- Burns, Samantha, LMHC. *Breaking Up & Bouncing Back*. Mineola, NY: Ixia Press, 2018.

- Sincero, Jen. *You Are A Badass*. Philadelphia, PA: Running Press, 2013.
- Website: THE BEST BRAIN POSSIBLE with Debbie Hampton. https://thebestbrainpossible.com/movie-help-mental-health-therapy/
- YouTube: If Someone Broke Your Heart -WATCH THIS | by Jay Shetty

Heartbreak Grief Overview

- Burns, Samantha, LMHC. *Breaking Up & Bouncing Back*. Mineola, NY: Ixia Press, 2018.
- Website: HELP ON HEALING FROM HEART-BREAK by Margarita Tartakovsky, M.S. https://psychcentral.com/blog/help-on-healing-from-heart-break/
- Website: WHAT YOU SHOULD KNOW ABOUT THE STAGES OF GRIEF by Kimberly Holland https://www.healthline.com/health/stages-of-grief
- Website: 7 STAGES OF GRIEVING A BREAK-UP by Suzanne Lachmann Psy.D. https://www.psychologytoday.com/us/blog/me-we/201406/the-7-stages-grieving-breakup

Chapter One: Shock

- Website: WHAT IS PSYCHOLOGICAL SHOCK? AND 5 TIPS FOR COPING by Alice

Boyes, Ph.D. https://www.psychologytoday.com/us/blog/in-practice/201803/what-is-psychological-shock-and-5-tips-coping

- Website: 7 WARNING SIGNS YOU ARE SUFFERING FROM EMOTIONAL SHOCK by Sheri Jacobson. https://www.harleytherapy.co.uk/counselling/7-warning-signs-acute-stress-reaction-emotional-shock.htm

- Website IN A STATE OF SHOCK AFTER A BREAKUP? HERE IS HOW TO MOVE FORWARD! https://www.withmyexagain.com/blog/state-of-shock-after-a-breakup/

- Website: BETTER HELP--Affordable, private online counseling. https://www.betterhelp.com/helpme/?utm_source=AdWords&utm_medium=Search_PPC_c&utm_term=relationship+counseling+free_e&utm_content=27017775010&network=g&placement=&target=&matchtype=e&utm_campaign=371722090&ad_type=text&adposition=&gclid=CjwKCAjw2uf2BRBpEiwA31VZ-jyRO6NC44lS0JsOOgKzQEiYVYY1-WogG6ggBkTIud8IJL5aSf6FB6vRoCyzIQAvD_BwE&not_found=1&gor=helpme

- Website: HOW DO YOU HEAL FROM THE SHOCK OF A SUDDEN BREAKUP? by Laurie Pawlick-Kienlen. https://howloveblossoms.com/how-to-heal-from-breakup-shock-of-breaking-up/

- Website: HOW TO GET OVER SOMEONE
WHO BLINDSIDED YOU, BECAUSE IT'S
NOT EASY by Christy Pina. https://www.elitedaily.
com/p/how-to-get-over-someone-who-blindsided-
you-because-its-not-easy-13167807
- Website: ACUTE STRESS DISORDER SYMP-
TOMS by John M. Grohol, Psy.D. https://psychcen-
tral.com/disorders/acute-stress-disorder-symptoms/
- Website: IMDB. https://www.imdb.com/title/
tt1000774/?ref_=ttfc_fc_tt

Chapter Two: Denial

- Westberg, Granger. *Good Grief*. Minneapolis, MN:
Fortress Press, 2011.
- Burns, Samantha. *Breaking Up & Bouncing Back*.
Mineola, New York: Ixia Press, 2018.
- Website: HOW TO STOP BEING IN DENIAL
ABOUT YOUR BREAKUP, BECAUSE WE'VE
ALL BEEN THERE by Christy Pina. https://
www.elitedaily.com/p/how-to-stop-being-in-de-
nial-about-your-breakup-because-weve-all-been-
there-13179266
- Website: 5 SIGNS YOU'RE IN DENIAL ABOUT
YOUR BREAKUP, ACCORDING TO EX-
PERTS by Rachel Shatto https://www.elitedaily.
com/p/5-signs-youre-in-denial-about-your-break-

up-according-to-experts-12609565
- Website: WHAT IS THE EMPTY CHAIR TECHNIQUE AND WHY DO THERAPISTS USE IT? by William Drake https://www.betterhelp.com/advice/therapy/wh at-is-the-empty-chair-technique-and-why-do-therapists-use-it/
- Website: COOL INTERVENTION #9: THE EMPTY CHAIR by Ryan Howes Ph.D. https://www.psychologytoday.com/us/blog/in-therapy/201001/cool-intervention-9-the-empty-chair-1
- Website: IMDB. https://www.imdb.com/title/tt1045658/?ref_=nv_sr_srsg_0/
- Website: OVEREATERS ANONYMOUS. https://oa.org/
- Website: ALCOHOLICS ANONYMOUS. https://www.aa.org/
- Website: NARCOTICS ANONYMOUS. https://www.na.org/
- Website: DEBTORS ANONYMOUS. https://debtorsanonymous.org/
- Website: GAMBLERS ANONYMOUS. http://www.gamblersanonymous.org/ga/conten t/about-us

Chapter Three: Anger

- Burton, Valorie. *Happy Women Live Better*. Eugene, Oregon: Harvest House Publishers, 2013.
- Walsh, Dr. Wendy. *The 30-day Love Detox*. New York, NY: Rodale Inc., 2013.

- Woodruff, Jessalyn. *Anger Management Best Practices Handbook*. Emereo Press.
- Carter, Les, Ph.D. and Frank Minirth, M.D. *The Anger Workbook-an interactive guide to anger management*. Nashville, TN: Thomas Nelson, Inc, 2012.
- Carlson Ph.D., Richard. *DON'T SWEAT THE SMALL STUFF...and it's all small stuff*. New York, NY: Hyperion, 1997.
- Lerner, Harriet, Ph.D. *The Dance of Anger*. New York, NY: William Morrow, 2014.
- Website: HOW TO MANAGE YOUR ANGER AFTER A BREAKUP by Sheri Jacobson. https://www.harleytherapy.co.uk/counselling/ manage-anger-after-breakup.htm
- Website: MINDFUL ANGER MANAGEMENT by Laura Harvey.https://www.huffpost.com/entry/anger-management_b_1462033
- Website: MINDFULNESS EXERCISES. https://mindfulnessexercises.com/
- Website: FANDANGO. https://www.fandango.com/waiting-to-exhale-42320/movie-overview

Chapter Four: Depression

- Thomson, Brian and Matt Broadway-Horner. *Managing Depression with CBT for Dummies*. Chichester, West Sussex: John Wiley & Sons, 2013.
- Website: https://www.psychologytoday.com/us/therapy-types/dialectical-behavior-therapy

- Website: NATIONAL SUICIDE PREVENTION LIFELINE. https://suicidepreventionlifeline.org/
- Website: WHAT HAPPENS WHEN A BREAK-UP BECOMES DEPRESSION? by Sarah Jacoby https://www.yahoo.com/lifestyle/happens-break-up-becomes-depression-224000974.html
- Website: AFTER A BREAKUP: PUTTING YOURSELF BACK TOGETHER by F. Diane Barth, L.C.S.W. https://www.psychologytoday.com/us/blog/the-couch/201911/after-breakup-putting-yourself-back-together
- Website: THERAPISTS EXPLAIN HOW TO AVOID DEPRESSION AFTER A BREAKUP by The Power of Positivity https://www.powerofpositivity.com/avoid-depression-after-breakup/
- Website: A BAD BREAKUP CAN TRIGGER A MENTAL HEALTH CONDITION by Sarah Bregel. https://www.instyle.com/beauty/health-fitness/depression-after-breakup
- Website: WHAT IS DIALECTICAL BEHAVIOR THERAPY (DBT)? by Leslie Riopel, MSc. https://positivepsychology.com/what-is-dialectial-behavior-therapy-dbt/
- Website: 9 SIGNS OF DEPRESSION IN WOMEN. https://www.powerofpositivity.com/signs-of-depression-in-women/
- Website: IMDB. https://www.imdb.com/title/tt0804497/?ref_=tt_urv

Chapter Five: Desperate for Answers and/or Contact

- Walsh, Dr. Wendy. *The 30-day Love Detox*. New York, NY: Rodale Inc., 2013.
- Burns, Samantha, LMHC. *Breaking Up & Bouncing Back*. Mineola, NY: Ixia Press, 2018.
- Elliott, Susan J. *Getting Past Your Breakup*. Cambridge, MA: Da Capo Press, 2009.
- Website: 12 REASONS WHY THE NO CONTACT RULE ALWAYS WORKS by Amelie Lee. https://www.lovepanky.com/love-couch/your-ex/why-the-no-contact-rule-works
- Website: SINGLE STRUGGLES: AFFECTION AND INTIMACY WITHDRAWALS by Charlotty Herman. https://www.hercampus.com/school/bu/single-struggles-affection-and-intimacy-withdrawals
- Website: WHAT HAPPENS TO YOUR BODY AFTER A BREAKUP, ACCORDING TO EXPERTS by Lily Rouff. https://www.elitedaily.com/p/what-happens-to-your-body-after-a-breakup-according-to-experts-7991528
- Website: WHY WE NEED CLOSURE FROM BROKEN RELATIONSHIPS by Mariana Bockarova, Ph.D. https://www.psychologytoday.com/us/blog/ro mantically-attached/201609/why-we-need-closure-broken-relationships
- Website: THE NO. 1 RULE EVERY GIRL NEEDS TO KNOW DURING A BREAKUP by

Akirah Robinson. https://www.glamour.com/story/breakup-no-contact-rule
- Website: 7 STAGES OF GRIEVING A BREAK-UP by Suzanne Lachmann Psy.D. https://www.psychologytoday.com/us/blog/me-we/201406/the-7-stages-grieving-breakup
- Website: IMDB. https://www.imdb.com/title/tt0093010/

Chapter Six: Acceptance

- Biegel, Gina M. *Be Mindful & Stress Free-50 Ways to Deal With Your Crazy Life*. Boulder, CO: Shambhala Publications, 2018
- Burns, Samantha, LMHC. *Breaking Up & Bouncing Back*. Mineola, NY: Ixia Press, 2018.
- Website: 8 OF THE REALITIES YOU MUST ACCEPT WHEN MENDING YOUR HEART AFTER A BREAKUP by Samantha Reynolds. https://www.elitedaily.com/dating/sex/8-of-the-realities-you-must-accept-when-mending-your-heart-after-a-breakup
- Website: A SIMPLE, ACTIONABLE GUIDE TO MOVING ON AFTER HEARTBREAK by Brittany Wong. https://www.huffpost.com/entry/a-simple-actionable-guide-to-moving-on-after-heartbreak_n_569e7eefe4b04c813761a22a
- Website: YOU AND ACCEPTANCE AFTER DIVORCE by Connie Wetzell and Michelle

RESOURCES

Borquez https://www.faithgateway.com/you-and-acceptance-after-divorce/

- Website: 6 STAGES OF ACCEPTANCE I WENT THROUGH AFTER MY DIVORCE by Divorcedmoms Staff. https://divorcedmoms.com/6-stages-of-acceptance-i-went-through-after-my-divorce/
- Website: IMDB. https://www.imdb.com/title/tt0250494/?ref_=fn_al_tt_1

Be the First
to Hear About
Other New Books
from Tanya Partee!

Sign up for announcements about
new and upcoming titles at:

www.lyfebydesign.net

Follow us on

#lyfebydesigncoach

Join us on

@lyfebydesigncoach